Becoming Georgia

I0894166

Becoming Georgia

From Revolution to Evolution

Georgia Morissette

Duo Editions 2026

Les Presses de l'Université d'Ottawa
University of Ottawa Press

Les Presses de l'Université d'Ottawa / University of Ottawa Press (PUO-UOP) is North America's flagship bilingual university press, affiliated to one of Canada's top research universities. PUO-UOP enriches the intellectual and cultural discourse of our increasingly knowledge-based and globalized world with peer-reviewed, award-winning books.

www.Press.uOttawa.ca

Library and Archives Canada Cataloguing in Publication

Title: Becoming Georgia : from revolution to evolution / Georgia Morissette.
Names: Morissette, Georgia, author.
Identifiers: Canadiana (print) 20260241776 | Canadiana (ebook) 20260241792 | ISBN 9780776647692 (hardcover) | ISBN 9780776647685 (softcover) | ISBN 9780776647708 (EPUB) | ISBN 9780776647715 (PDF))
Subjects: LCSH: Morissette, Georgia. | LCSH: Women educators—Canada—Biography. | LCSH: Educators—Canada—Biography. | LCGFT: Autobiographies.
Classification: LCC LA2325.M674 A3 2026 | DDC 370.92—dc23

Legal Deposit: Third Quarter 2026
Library and Archives Canada

© University of Ottawa Press 2026
All rights reserved

No part of this publication may be reproduced or transmitted in any form or by any means, or stored in a database and retrieval system, without prior permission.

Production Team

Copy editing	Tanina Drvar and Guy Lazure
Proofreading	Robbie McCaw
Typesetting	Peter Handley
Cover design	Dany Lagueux
Cover image	Portrait photograph by Jean-Marc Carisse

uOttawa

PUO-UOP gratefully acknowledges the funding support of the University of Ottawa, the Government of Canada, the Canada Council for the Arts, the Ontario Arts Council and the Government of Ontario.

Canada | Canada Council for the Arts | Conseil des arts du Canada | Ontario Arts Council | Conseil des arts de l'Ontario | an Ontario government agency | un organisme du gouvernement de l'Ontario | Ontario

Table of Contents

List of Figures

First Foreword

Life can only be understood backwards; but it must be lived forwards.
– Søren Kierkegaard

READING SOMEONE'S MEMOIRS is a sacred and honouring process, as it is like opening a secret diary, allowing the reader to see into the deepest, most personal moments of the author's life. A special bond is formed between the writer and the reader, as we are invited into an unique and complex microcosm. *Memoirs*—a genre derived from the Latin word *memoria*—is one of the most personal forms of autobiographical literature, not just a chronicle of a life, but an artistic act of remembering, interpreting, and recording, that helps us to understand how individual fates are intertwined with historical events, and to grasp the universal, yet unique, experiences of human life.

As the cliché goes, everyone's life is a novel. That is why memoirs have invaluable significance. They are a historical source that complements official history by presenting, through the perspective of an eyewitness, how the writer experienced the storms of history, in this case the Hungarian Revolution of 1956. The author is also part of a journey of reflexive self-discovery, through which the reader can also be enriched with a unique, yet universal philosophy of life. This genre is a special treasure of storytelling, I could even say, a universal legacy, as bridges are built between generations and cultures, passing on the experiences and wisdom of predecessors.

Georgia's book is written with memories that are both sweet and painful, and on each page a smouldering spark of love for life is ignited, even in the shadow of tragedies and difficulties. This book presents an exceptionally beautiful but difficult life journey, in which we witness how a fragile, childlike personality experiencing difficult times changes into a strong, self-aware, fully self-loving adult woman who experienced many traumas.

For me, these memoirs present the entire process of individuality blossoming through Georgia's life. The intervening testimonies of the children, grandchildren, and friends weave the fabric of collective experience into the individual's memory. In my view, this book is a polyphonic choir, where individuality reveals its true self to the reader in the meeting of many voices and in the echoes of loving remembrance.

Another special feature of the book is that this story is not just a single, solitary stream of memories. As such, it is not the narrative voice of the classic monologue that dominates the text. Rather, the interruption of the narrative, when the author's recollections reach their deepest, most personal point, breaks the story up in several cases, as if a mirror were falling into small pieces, in order to create an even richer picture not only of the memoirist, but also of the environment and the era in which she lived.

It was a great experience and honour for me to have read these memoirs, as I have become richer with true life wisdom. Georgia's book is proof that love, family, and perseverance do indeed enable us to find our own inner voice in a foreign land, without forgetting our roots. These memoirs are about the triumph of human self-realization, proving that, even on the longest and most difficult journey, only love can be the best navigator.

Anikó Zsuzsanna Antal
Author of *A holdarcú asszony* (The Woman with the Face of the Moon), *Önmozaik* (Self-Mosaic), *Lélekszimfónia* (Symphony of the Soul), and other books.

Second Foreword

GEORGIA HAS BEEN in my life for sixty-seven years now. In this book, you will share in the tragic and the magic of her unique life journey. The magic will tell of our lives together, and the tragic will speak of escape from a homeland at age ten, and of the trials and tribulations of a Hungarian refugee/immigrant family adjusting to a new life in Canada.

You will participate in our first meeting as young twelve-year-old kids. You will be surprised as to why we developed feelings for each other in the first days of school in our Grade 7 class. As we got to know each other, I saw and felt that this girl was as beautiful inside as she was outside. And as the oldest boy in a dysfunctional family scarred by infidelity, alcoholism, and abandonment, I owe the greatest debt of gratitude to serendipity, common sense, and nurture for having placed this woman on my path and having given me the wisdom to build a relationship and co-create a family with her.

Over the fifty-eight years of our marriage, Georgia has taught me and shown me in so many ways how to know myself and fulfill my potential. She is a positive, giving, caring, intelligent, courageous, and persevering woman. And she did it all by following the example of her parents. She was the extra caring mother I never had, and a model for our three children, Chad, Wade, and Alanis, who have truly benefited from her constant love and support.

All this to say that I believe if you speak from the heart, it is impossible for anyone not to hear you.

Enjoy the trip!

Alan Morissette

Dedication

THIS BOOK IS dedicated to my husband, Alan, who supported me throughout the writing of my memoirs. He has been the love of my life for fifty-eight years.

This book is also dedicated to our amazing three children, whom we deeply love and who are so vital to us both, as well as our seven grandchildren, with whom we not only share regular communication but also a profound connection.

I so appreciate the many friends and even strangers who care and who impact our lives; to these wonderful people, I also dedicate this book.

Finally, I dedicate my memoirs to all the people who have had to escape their homeland to experience true freedom.

Acknowledgements

WHAT A FABULOUS journey these memoirs have been.

It was such a gift to have my dear husband, Alan, by my side to remind me to share, and to help with many aspects of creation. I keep saying that he should be the co-author of this book, but he insists that it is my story, my memoirs. Alan's many hours of research into our one hundred photo albums to select the photos, and his assistance in composing, proofreading, and bringing new ideas have been such a gift to both this book and to me. All in all, I am so grateful to him for being the love of my life and my sweetheart husband for fifty-eight years.

Our three children have definitely been amazing over the many years. They are all in their fifties now. They have always kept in touch and enhanced and enriched our lives with their presence, their time, and their ongoing love.

Also, our seven cherished grandchildren who, even though some of them are in their twenties, respond on a regular basis when I connect with them or even initiate the connection.

Our wonderful family and friendship circle have shared ideas and friendly moments that have encouraged me to keep writing. My sister, Kati Alexandra, who has always been my best girlfriend, and Jacquie Morgan, who is like a sister to me as well, have both helped jog my memory regarding meaningful past events. I am so fortunate to have a sibling with whom I share a very special connection and bond. We have been there for each other through thick and thin. When she was little, she would often tattle on me, which sometimes caused a rift. However, the minute she started to like a boy around age twelve, we have gotten along well each and every decade of our lives, have supported each other, cheered each other on, and have had fun experiences together. She is definitely a gift and a giver to me and to so many people around her.

I have also been fortunate to have other people who have jumped in to help along the way. Thank you to Nicole MacDonald, who shared many wonderful aspects to include in the narrative. Nicole spent a great deal of time on how to best express my memories. Cheryl Bauman helped with so many of the ideas and used her computer skills to increase my knowledge on writing memoirs. Tara Shannon shared her own experience of having written a book to enrich my own.

I am extremely grateful for all the recognition that the various programs I have created have gained. I would like to take this opportunity to thank the many magazines, local newspapers, television networks, award committees, community centres, and retirement home activity directors for believing and promoting community wellness with me over the years. I truly appreciate the support they have shown throughout my continued involvement. The wonderful lifestyle of daily healthy eating and exercise I have learned along the way has served me well. My ability to teach chair yoga to seniors, even at my senior age, is both a joy and fulfillment.

I have been very fortunate to have found the perfect publisher for these memoirs, with an amazing group who has made this one of the best collaborative experiences ever. Lara, Danika, Mireille, Maryse, and Guy, I have nothing but respect and appreciation for your expertise, knowledge, patience, and communication skills. This professional group with their individual talents of leadership, creativity, and editing ideas has made this venture ideal. I could not have asked for a better team to work with.

My go-to saying is: "You can't be grateful and unhappy at the same time." I choose to be grateful.

Introduction

YOUR PAST CERTAINLY need not determine your present or your future. Yet it does, at times, and comes back to haunt you. And while it is often advised to live in the moment, there are occasions in one's life that force us to revisit and reflect on impactful or traumatic memories. And these tragic events of the past can, and often do, influence the speed of one's personal growth and development.

This is what these memoirs are all about.

As I approached my mid-seventies, I started flirting with the idea of writing my life story and the lessons I have learned along the way. My grandchildren also regularly enquired about my past and requested on multiple occasions to learn more about their family history, which is empowering.

But this is how it all began.

The year was 2020. While we were confined to our homes because of the COVID-19 pandemic, I was reminded of my life as a child. In 1956, at the age of ten, I experienced a whole different type of lockdown—one that resulted in unimaginable consequences if you chose to disobey any state regulations.

Two years after we first went into lockdown, rules started to relax, case numbers dwindled, and much of the world opened up again. Everywhere you went, whether it was at a grocery store or on the street, you were greeted with smiles by those who chose to take the masks off. Wearing masks became a choice, except in care facilities, and a renewed sense of freedom and joy was palpable.

Very quickly, however, devastating news of a distant war became the latest television headline. Ukraine was under attack and COVID became yesterday's news. Our screens were filled with images of families, young and old, fleeing their homes in search of safety, suddenly faced with an unwelcome threat. Under the rule of authoritarian leader Vladimir Putin, Russia had invaded Ukraine, clearly intent on annexing the country. As I watched families hiding, waiting, and fleeing, and seeing the photos and videos of children with their little suitcases, I wondered how they would cope with their trauma.

The invasion of Ukraine took me back to the start of the Hungarian Revolution in my childhood city of Budapest. My family and I were faced with a life-altering decision, in much the same way these families were. Should we stay or should we go? As I travelled back in time, I remembered how the ten-year-old girl I had been made sense of her life and the events that unfolded around her. To deal with the seriousness of the moment, life became an adventure-filled quest. I hoped as much for the Ukrainian children.

One might think that clandestinely escaping my country would have permanently traumatized or scarred me.

But it did not.

It was my arrival in Canada as a refugee that diminished my freedom and separated me from my extraverted self for many years. It was not until I was an adult that I faced an abrupt turning point that shook me in a powerful way. Little did I know at the time that this would be a life-defining moment—the day my authentic self would finally be set free. I was reminded that I am a strong, powerful woman. My altruistic self also came through and became evident.

To this day, I strive to help others shine while also reminding them to acknowledge, accept, and adjust.

My goal, in writing this book, is, therefore, to excavate my authentic self by investigating the treasures and traumas of my past. To reflect on my journey and inspire others to understand and empathize with the plight of refugees and immigrants. To bring hope to those who are or have been impacted by the traumatic personal upheaval caused by external forces.

Travel back with me in time to relive the events that unfolded throughout the Hungarian Revolution and my own personal evolution. Perhaps along the way, you too will experience growth or transformation and rediscover your own true self.

1

Into the Fire: My Father's Jewish Family in the Second World War

If you want the present to be different from the past, study the past.
– Baruch Spinoza

As I BEGAN writing, it seemed important to provide historical context on my home country of Hungary in the years leading up to what I experienced as a ten-year-old child. But also, to share what my parents lived through, which led to, and accelerated their decision to leave Hungary during the revolution of 1956. Since my parents were very private people, even to their own children, it was not until my seventies that I learned key details of their lives prior to my birth. I am incredibly grateful to a close family friend, Vera Kovesi, who shared her knowledge of my parents' past with me. This compelled me to draw a portrait of the historical situation they faced prior to their departure from Hungary.

My father, Imre Feuerstein, and his family owned an office supply wholesale company in Budapest. Perhaps this is why I have always loved pens, pencils, paper, and writing pads of all kinds. His family were well-to-do businessmen of Jewish origin. My mother, Nadinia, came from a strict Catholic family. After she graduated from high school, she landed a job at my grandparents' store as a clerk. That is where my parents met and fell in love in 1941, in the middle of a world war and in a country allied with Nazi Germany, which, ironically, protected its important and prosperous Jewish community for as long as it could. If there was a significant age gap between my parents—my father was thirty-two years old at the time and my mother only eighteen—this did not matter to them.

When the Germans invaded the Soviet Union in 1941, the Hungarian government decided to conscript around fifty thousand Jewish men into "labour battalions" that were sent to dig trenches and clear mines on the Eastern Front. It would seem that my father's brothers, Sandor and Gyorgy, were among the number. It is not clear to me how my father managed to escape, but I heard stories of him hiding in a closet of their apartment. Only a little over ten percent of these men came back to Hungary in the spring and summer of 1943. My uncle Gyorgy appears to have been one of the lucky few. Sensing that the loyalty of their ally was dwindling as the war was ending, the Nazis decided to occupy Hungary in March 1944. Most of the Jewish-owned businesses in Budapest were then immediately and forcibly closed, including my father's family office supply store. My mother, who was determined to help the family survive, tried to save whatever valuable business assets she could. She also helped my paternal grandparents with food and anything else she could find. My parents lived in a beautiful apartment in Szent István Park, a wealthy neighbourhood where many Jewish people lived, which would have been lost if my mother had not taken good care of it in their absence through the last year of the war.

Although Hungarian authorities managed to suspend the mass deportation planned for the summer of 1944 of Budapest's Jewish community, which neared three hundred thousand at that point, the Nazis regained control of the city and began to round up Jews from the ghettos in October and November. Within a couple of months, nearly one hundred thousand of them were sent either on foot or by rail to the border checkpoint of Hegyeshalom (today on the northwestern edge of Hungary, on the border with Austria and Slovakia), to build a defensive line called the Southeastern Wall. Those who survived the winter and the inhumane living and working conditions—suffering from exhaustion, starvation, disease, and under constant threat of execution—either continued their death march across Austria or were placed on trains and ships bound for concentration camps across the Reich. That was the last my father saw of his younger brother, Gyorgy. From what our family friend Vera recalls, my father was then enrolled in the forced labour service army (*munkaszolgálat*) and was sent, like most Jewish men who remained, to a camp somewhere in Hungary. Imre only managed to return to Budapest at the end of the war. As for his parents, I do not know what happened to his father, Izidor, but I can only imagine the worst. It appears that his mother, Rozalia (Roza) Spitzer Feuerstein, survived the pogroms and made it through the devastating siege of Budapest by the Soviets, who encircled and bombed the city for nearly two months until they completed its occupation on February 13, 1945. She died on March 10 and was buried in Budapest's Jewish cemetery.

* * *

Once the war was over, and while my father was still mourning the loss of his family, my parents were married. That very day, on May 31, he chose to renounce the pain and death brought on by his Jewish heritage and, at my mother's insistence, converted to Catholicism in the hopes of protecting both himself and his future family from religious discrimination and antisemitism. I was born a little over a year after, on July 14, 1946, the day that marked the fall of the Bastille and the start of the French Revolution. My husband Alan always says that this special day exemplified me as I too, stormed into this world, as a force of positive change.

1.1. Georgia's father, Imre Feuerstein, unknown date and location.
Source: Family Collection.

1.2. Georgia's uncle, Gyorgy Feuerstein, unknown date and location.
Source: Family Collection.

1.3. Georgia's older uncle, Sandor Feuerstein, unknown date and location.
Source: Family Collection.

1.4. Georgia's parents and maternal grandparents, Katalin and Mihaly, Budapest, May 31, 1945.
Source: Family Collection.

1.5. Georgia's parents, Nadinia and Imre Feuerstein, Budapest, May 31, 1945.
Source: Family Collection.

2 Early Years: Before the Revolution (1946–1956)

IT IS SAID that when you dig deep inside, it all comes back to you. These memoirs are a journey filled with surprising discoveries about my original self. My memories of what it was like to be a little girl during that early period, before the onslaught of a profoundly disturbing disruption in my life, live on forever in my mind as a unique time spent in my homeland and my childhood home. And yet, the writing experience unlocked recollections and insights that came as surprises.

As a child, I took things more lightly and, on many levels, experienced the turmoil that gripped Hungary during those years as an adventure. This innocent view of the world shielded me and gave me an advantage in surviving the surrounding chaos and uncertainty.

We lived on the third floor of a very nice building in a central neighbourhood of the city. As we entered the apartment, there was a small powder room on the right. As hard as it might seem to believe today, at the time we used pieces of newspaper as toilet paper. Across the hallway, there were some cupboards. As I recall, there was a pantry, and after that the kitchen with a veranda and a little balcony. Off the kitchen was a small bedroom. Walking back to the front door, there were two doors with translucent glass that led to a small living area. To the left of that, there was the main bathroom, which had a second door that led into my parents' bedroom. At the end of the hallway, there was a large room with several windows, a big dining table, a wide couch, and a radio. On this couch, our parents would sit and read books to my four-year-old sister Kati and me. I used to play Canasta with my mother and father in this living room and recall listening to music and news on the radio. There was also a closet with shelves. Not clothing shelves, but shelves on which I could place my belongings, a little doll for instance or a little pillow that I used to carry around under my arm as a safety blanket while simultaneously sucking on my thumb (a soothing habit that my mother unsuccessfully tried to stop by putting some horrible tasting liquid on my thumb).

I loved looking out the open window and watching life on the street below and in the park in front. To the left of the window, there was another park and a swimming area. Across from that park was the Danube River. And if you walked

2.1. Georgia, at seven months old, Budapest, 1947.
Source: Family Collection.

2.2. Georgia, at four years old, Budapest, 1950.
Source: Family Collection.

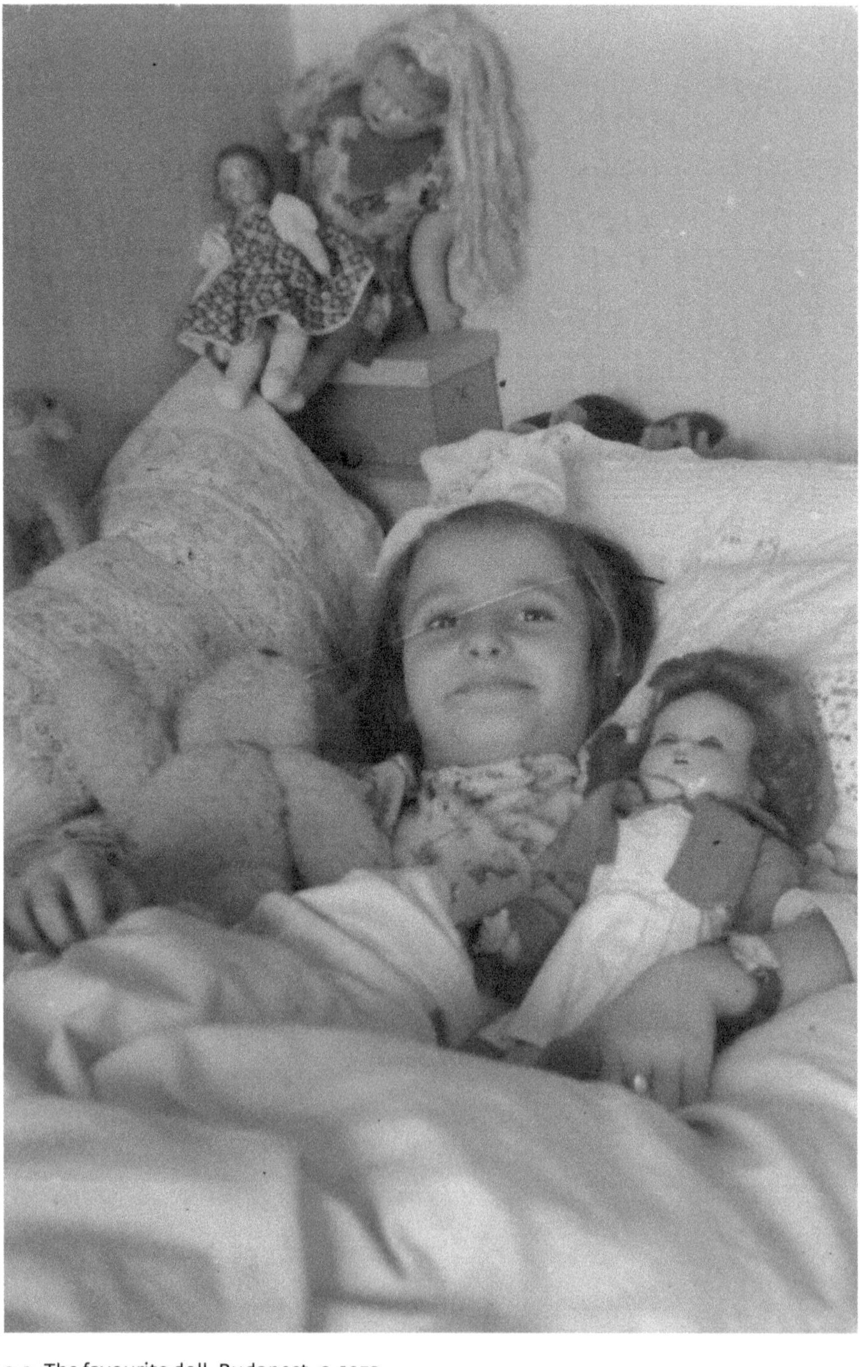

2.3. The favourite doll, Budapest, c. 1952.
Source: Family Collection.

across the park, a little boat would take you to Margaret Island, filled with beautiful walkways, a large swimming area, lovely restaurants, beautiful plants, and flowers along the pathways. That was a very special outing we did every now and then as a family. We sometimes went to the park to play. My parents played tennis at a nearby public court, and I remember being the ball girl.

In the hallway by the front door was a small icebox, which kept food and beverages fresh and safe. The only problem was that we had to buy a new block of ice every day, since it would melt by the next morning. As you walked down the hall to the kitchen, there was a big sink with four legs, a stove, and a countertop. My mother woke up at five thirty every morning, and an hour later she was home from the market, where she had bought all the groceries for that day. Every now and then, usually towards the beginning of the month, she would come home with a live chicken and tie one of its legs to the bottom of the sink. The chicken would run around the kitchen until we killed it and cooked it for supper. At the time, my grandmother was living with us, but I had first witnessed her rather brutal method of wringing a chicken's neck before preparing it during our summer visits to my grandparents' countryside farm—a spectacle that made the city girl in me quite glad I was never responsible for helping her cook.

"I don't think I'm going to get married," I would tell my mother, "unless I can ask my husband to wring the neck of the chicken, because I won't."

I just could not see myself doing that kind of meal preparation. It is a wonder that after all this I still eat chicken to this day and that I have not become a vegetarian. It was during those summer holidays that I discovered the difference between city and country, and the gap that separated them. Many of the village women wore scarves around their heads, and from what I remember, there was not that much camaraderie between the city folk and the country folk.

* * *

Back then, I was enrolled in gymnastics class on Thursday nights. I truly loved it. I fondly recall that on the way home I would get a scoop of ice cream from this little restaurant. The two paired well, gymnastics followed by a special treat.

As I think of this, I wonder why I was never taught how to swim, a sport that has always been extremely popular and widely practised in Hungary. I was very good at gymnastics and was even asked to pose for a health book promoting activities for young children. The photographers wanted to get a picture of me bending my spine. Being just a little girl, I was in my bathing suit bottom for the picture doing a bridge pose. I was then asked when I stood up to do it again, this time pulling the panties down a little bit more. I still remember saying firmly: "No, thank you!"

2.4. and 2.5. Gymnastics lessons, Budapest, c. 1954–1955.
Source: Family Collection.

I also remember loving downhill skiing. We would head over to Buda, across the river on the opposite side of Pest, and take a tram up to the foot of the hill. Since there were no ski lifts at the time, we had to hike up to the top in our boots to be able to ski down. Then climb back up again and whisk down again. Climb-ski-repeat! I would scream for people to get out of my way as I barrelled down the hill. I really enjoyed these ski excursions with my parents and quickly became accomplished at skiing.

If I was quite eager to participate in sports and physical activities, something that was highly valued, strongly encouraged, and heavily subsidized by the Communist state, I was much more reluctant to learn languages, as my parents wanted me to. I was simply not interested in any other language besides Hungarian, especially since I was already forced to learn Russian in school. To this day I cannot say a word in Russian even though I studied it for at least three years.

Reading was also a challenge for me. I had managed to keep my marks up until Grade 2 when my mother once checked how my reading was progressing. I still remember that precise moment. Just as we finished a story, she took three or four words and wrote them down on the edge of a newspaper. She asked me what

2.6. Georgia skiing with her mother, Budapest, c. 1954.
Source: Family Collection..

those words were. I could not read a single one of them! My mother and my teacher figured out that I was not a good reader at all, but that I had an excellent memory. I would memorize what I heard in class during the day and then repeat it back to my mother at night.

★★★

I was always a bit of a tomboy, and even at that early age, boys were a part of my life. A boy named István, which translates as "Steven" in English, liked me and bought me a little pot top for my toy pot, with which I used to do a little pretend cooking. He also visited me at Easter because, in Hungary, if a boy liked a girl, he would come to her house with a perfume bottle, knock on her door, and when she answered, he would sprinkle some perfume on her head. In exchange, the boy would ask for a kiss and a coloured egg. This religious ritual is associated with fertility, healing, and the cleansing rites in the Roman Catholic tradition. On a more unpleasant note, there were some boys who fired little guns at me with tiny rocks in them. I remember the stones hitting my heels, which was very painful. I was scared to come home after school whenever I saw them. One day, my dad asked me why I came home late and I told him what these boys were doing. Sure enough, they were in front of my apartment building again the next evening. However, this time my father was also there. Never revealing who he was, he reprimanded them and warned them angrily that if they picked on me or were ever seen in our neighbourhood again, they would be reported to the police and punished. Weeks later, I saw them close to the front door of my apartment. As they were eyeing me, I said: "You do know that the man who told you to stop this is watching you every single time I come home. I would be very well behaved if I were you."

They left. I never told them it was my father.

* * *

In movies about Communist countries, you often see younger children wearing blue scarves and older ones wearing red scarves. These meant that you were part of the Communist youth movement. Well, that was all right in my mind at the time. A colourful scarf went with everything. I remember one incident with this uniform that began to open my eyes, however. This was not simply a cute uniform we had to wear. It bore significance. This was revealed to me at class picture time. As for any school photo, I sat down in front of the photographer, smiled, tilted my head the way I was told, and so on. Everything was going well until suddenly my teacher just about lunged at me. Moving next to the photographer, she yelled:

"Put that away!"

Puzzled, I asked:

"What am I to put away?"

I had received a little gold cross necklace for my first communion, which I decided to wear for picture day. Since I had to wear my scarf, I decided to hang my gold cross over it. My teacher, having realized the necklace was showing, again barked:

"Put that necklace away and don't let me see it again!"

2.7. First communion, Budapest, c. 1953.
Source: Family Collection.

In the excitement of the moment, with the photographer waiting and my teacher throwing a fit, I did not know what was happening, nor why. But that is when I began to realize that I was not free to do the things I wanted to do and be who I wanted to be. I remember quickly tucking the cross under my collar, deeply upset by this whole incident. The school picture has my gold necklace hanging from the side because, since I could not tuck it in properly, I decided instead to flip it over to the right side of my blouse for everyone to see.

This incident, along with a few similar events, revealed to the little eight-year-old I was that my city was no longer the friendly place I had grown up in. When I walked to church on Sundays, I could not proudly hold my prayer book. I had to hide it because if I was caught displaying or practising my religion (which ran against Communist principles), my parents stood an excellent chance of losing their jobs. And since their jobs already did not provide enough income for the family, I certainly did not want to jeopardize my parents' employment.

I remember that my mother did not like the new rules imposed on religious celebrations in Budapest. On the day of my first communion, one of my mother's friends (who later escaped to Austria) advised her to only dress me up in the white dress and white veil once at the church, since we did not have a car. It was dangerous to be seen walking down the street dressed in such a way because you never knew who was watching you from the Communist Party. If you were seen by a party member, you would lose your job. As I remember, that is where my mother drew the line and expressed her agitation:

"This is a big day in my daughter's life, and I don't care what happens as a result. She is wearing her white dress from home to the church. And if anything happens, I'll just suffer the consequences. I have reached my limits with these restrictions."

⋆ ⋆ ⋆

What I was beginning to notice was my parents' growing feelings of frustration and disapproval with the rules that were now being imposed by the government. This was particularly salient with my father's family stationery store. For the Soviets, these types of businesses were considered privately owned capitalistic enterprises, which the Communist regime did not allow. My parents had a friend who was a member of the Communist Party. One day, he went up to my mom and warned her:

"Your husband's name is on the prohibited list of private ownership. Once they find out about this, they will walk in and seize the store and the business. They just seal the door. It is no longer yours. It becomes government property."

The Feuersteins' office supply store was indeed taken over by the Soviets, but my parents were rehired as employees by the Communists, who needed their expertise. This came as a harsh warning.

My grandmother was not as lucky. She did not receive any forewarning about her business.

Since Hungary is landlocked, our largest body of water, Lake Balaton, is regarded by many as the "Hungarian Sea." There were beautiful resorts along the shores of the lake, and my grandparents owned a restaurant nearby. It was next to the train station, making it an ideal place for people to enjoy on their holidays. As many people did not own cars after the war, travelling by train was a popular mode of transportation. The station was within walking distance from the beach, and the restaurant became a great place to stop for a meal and entertainment before taking the train back home.

During those years, we used to go there to swim on weekends. We would take the train on Saturday morning and head straight to the restaurant. I remember that whenever we went, I would ping on the black grand piano that was there for people to play and entertain the guests. The piano was already taking centre stage in my life, as it would so often do in the future. Back in the city, I would hear the world-famous Jewish pianist Annie Fischer, who lived in the same building as us, play on the floor above our apartment. Listening to her practice may have inspired me to have our three children learn piano as their very first instrument in Canada.

One day, at the restaurant, just as I was getting ready to tap away, my parents yelled:

"Don't touch the piano!"

I was dumbfounded. I always played the piano when we visited.

"What's the matter?"

My parents, both in a panic, replied:

"Don't you see the seal on the piano?"

"What seal?"

I had nearly torn off the piece of tape over the lid. I had thought nothing of it. And yet, this tape was nothing like gift wrap. I still remember my parents reading it to me:

"GOVERNMENT PROPERTY! YOU WILL BE PROSECUTED IF OPENED."

In other words, had I stripped off that tape, the piano would have been taken away and there could have been serious repercussions for my grandparents. Shortly after this episode, my grandparents' restaurant was seized by the Hungarian state, and they moved in with us in our Budapest apartment. That piano was still there when my husband Alan and I visited the restaurant several decades later.

***

Another incident that made me feel insecure about where my country was heading at the time happened when my mother went to a parent-teacher interview. Back then, I was still a straight A student working very hard in the Grade 4 program. I was focused on my studies and there were no distractions yet (like boys). The teacher acknowledged my excellent grades but added: "That's a real pity." Of course, this remark caught my mother's attention. She was not sure what the teacher meant by that, so she asked her.

"You know, if you're looking at a near perfect report card, what is the matter or the pity? What is this conversation about?"

The teacher responded:

"Well, Georgia won't be able to pursue her studies beyond Grade 8."

"Why not?" my mother enquired.

"Well, wasn't your husband the owner of a stationery store before the children came along? That classifies you as rich, since you owned private property. Because of that, your daughter will only be allowed to go up to Grade 8; she will then have to work in a factory."

That meant that, despite being a stellar student, I would not have the freedom to continue my education in the school system. By the early 1950s, the Soviet Communist regime had begun its campaign against private ownership and capitalism. Children of bourgeois families were forced to work in factories and were forbidden to pursue a secondary education. The teacher tried to sugarcoat the news by saying that there were all kinds of benefits and possibilities for advancement when working in a factory. But she was clearly promoting the party.

For my parents, this was no longer about government measures designed to erase class distinctions and privileges in order to level the playing field for all, at the cost of civil liberties. They accepted the loss of their business. They accepted the daily struggles. But this was different. This was their daughter's future.

* * *

The Soviets had master lists of Hungarians who had owned private businesses. When your name was added to the list, you were driven out of the country and exiled to an unknown and undisclosed location. Since we were on this list, it was only a matter of time before they came to get our family. Stories circulated regarding the people who were arrested. All we knew was that if they came to your door, that meant goodbye, and you were never to be seen again.

I remember enjoying the 1977 movie *The Car*. In the film, a black car that was possessed eliminated anybody in its way. That movie kind of reminded me of what was happening in 1950s Hungary, but the Soviets were using a small truck instead of a car because there was more room for people to be abducted.

Among the many rumours circulating, one was that they would kill you. Another was that, if you led a comfortable life, lived in a nice apartment in a nice neighbourhood, you would now get a taste of what it was like to be a labourer. They would take you to a village and make you live in a hut, taking every belonging away from you, except for the clothes on your back. You would be forced to leave your office desk job and toil in the fields alongside the peasants. It was said that the reason these people never came back was because they were just too ashamed to face their old friends again. I do not know if any of those rumours were true, but there were people that my own family knew for whom the car came and who never returned.

By then, we were no longer rich or even financially comfortable. My father was most likely unemployed—how else could he have had time to pick me up from school in the middle of the afternoon—while my mother worked for a newspaper company, a prestigious job, perhaps, but the salary was barely enough to feed a family of four. She used to get paid on the third of every month. For about a week after that, we had a bit of money on hand and could eat pretty nice meals. After the tenth of the month, our lifestyle would begin to suffer and decline. We might occasionally get a small piece of meat, but for the most part we had to ration.

I noticed that my mother, who always wore her gold wedding band, did not seem to have it as the month progressed. As I became more aware of jewelry, I remember asking her one day, "Mom, could you tell me why for one or two weeks you always have your wedding band on, and then for the rest of the month you don't? What do you do with it? Do you get it cleaned?"

"Oh, well, you can come with me next time I go about my business."

And so, when the time of the month came for her wedding ring to come off again, I accompanied her to a pawn shop.

She had made an arrangement with the pawnbroker. She would rebuy the ring every month at an additional cost, as soon as she got paid on the third. The only way that she could make do for the rest of the month was by getting some money for her ring.

That is how rich we were.

If our feet hurt because we had outgrown our shoes, we could not simply go shopping for a new pair; we would have to wait for months. When the bed sheets ripped, we would patch them up. It got to a point where there was not a complete sheet available. Some had so many patches you could not lie down on a straight piece. If we saved enough money, then we might be able to afford new sheets six months later. We did not go out to a restaurant for someone's birthday. We could barely afford a decent meal at home. I did not even know what a restaurant was at that age, except for my grandmother's.

And so, because of our supposed well-to-do life, because of where we lived, and because we came from a "capitalist" family, I would not be able to attend high school and we would lose everything, which was not much at the time.

We also knew that the proverbial black vehicle was on the lookout for our family. However, we did not know when our turn would come. Where were we on that list? Number one, one thousand, five thousand? We only knew that our names were there.

Now that I think back on my parents' lives, and the things they told me over the years, they should have had grey hair or no hair at all left by their forties. I often wondered why they were such nervous people, and now that I revisit this time, I think I have finally truly understood.

One evening, my mother and father had just tucked us into bed—it would have been around eight o'clock. Then suddenly they heard "it"—and by "it," I mean THE CAR.

Hearing unusual commotion below, I got out of bed and peeked out the window. There "it" was. When "it" comes to your building and you know that you are on the list, the fear is as unimaginable as it is indescribable. There is no running away, no escaping.

I watched as government officials entered the building. I heard the elevator come up. Our apartment was on the third floor. We had lived there long enough to know exactly where the elevator was stopping. It stopped on our floor. My parents, shaking, held each other tight, trying to keep it together. We heard the Communist agents come out of the elevator, the door clanging shut behind them, their footsteps approaching. My parents were already whispering their goodbyes. They did not even care anymore, it was done, their fate was sealed.

The bell rang.

But it was the bell from across the hall. Those people were never seen again. For us, that was a turning point.

By then, it was the year 1956. My parents weighed their options. Anyone who has ever contemplated leaving their home country knows just how difficult it is. It is the place where you grew up, where your relatives are, where you made friends and built memories, maybe even fell in love for the first time; it is the language you first learned to speak and read. And yet, given the circumstances of our life in Budapest, my parents began to plan an escape while going on about their lives. I still went to gymnastics on Monday and Thursday nights, and I continued to take English and piano lessons on the other nights, where I recall throwing temper tantrums until my parents finally let me quit. One fall evening, as my parents came to pick me up from gymnastics class, the atmosphere in the neighbourhood felt totally different. Typically, after gymnastics, we would always stop at a coffee house for a scoop of ice cream. That was my big treat at the beginning of every month. But that one time, I remember the place overflowing and the streets crowded with people protesting. I remember thinking that I had never seen this kind of gathering before. What was going on? What was happening? Was everything okay?

The revolution had begun.

* * *

The memories of this tumultuous period of the fall of 1956 were shared with me later in life by my parents and friends of theirs who had lived through it. As Hungarian national identity resurfaced, university students decided they had had enough of Soviet oppression and began to call for the end of dictatorial one-party rule and the withdrawal of Soviet troops from Hungary, while demanding political and economic reforms. On October 23, they protested in the streets of Budapest to the resounding chants of patriotic anthems and "RUSSIANS GO HOME!" Marching to Parliament Square, the crowd swelled from fifty thousand to over two hundred thousand, with factory workers now forming the majority. Along the way, Hungarian flags stripped of their Communist symbols began to appear on apartment balconies, and red star placards were taken down. When protesters tore down the statue of Stalin and stormed the state radio station, the peaceful demonstration quickly escalated into an armed insurrection. The secret police (ÁVH) began to shoot at the crowd, and the rebels fired back. With Hungarian troops overwhelmed, the Red Army was called in.

After a week of massive strikes and heavy fighting in the streets, which led to the destruction of several buildings around the capital, as well as the burning of many Soviet tanks, the reformist government of Imre Nagy made some concessions to the people (free multi-party elections, withdrawal of Soviet troops), which brought calm back to the city. But just as the revolution appeared to have won, the Kremlin decided to impose its authority and crush the uprising. On November 4, 1956, we woke up to the Red Army occupying the city and to a new government put in place by Moscow. Our short moment of freedom had come to a brutal end.

To this day, I remember seeing the Soviet tanks roll into the streets of Budapest from our apartment. Stunned and awed at the same time, I sat and watched all day as hundreds of tanks passed underneath the windows with foot soldiers alongside wearing war helmets. I recall being horrified and asking my parents what was happening. They said the Soviets were coming to stop the university students from revolting. Ultimately, the Hungarian people were not supported by Western powers, who were not willing to get involved in Eastern Europe, and who were preoccupied by the international incident of the Suez Crisis.

The revolution officially ended on November 7, and by mid-December approximately two hundred thousand Hungarians—approximately two percent of the country's population—had sought refuge in other countries.

Including my family.

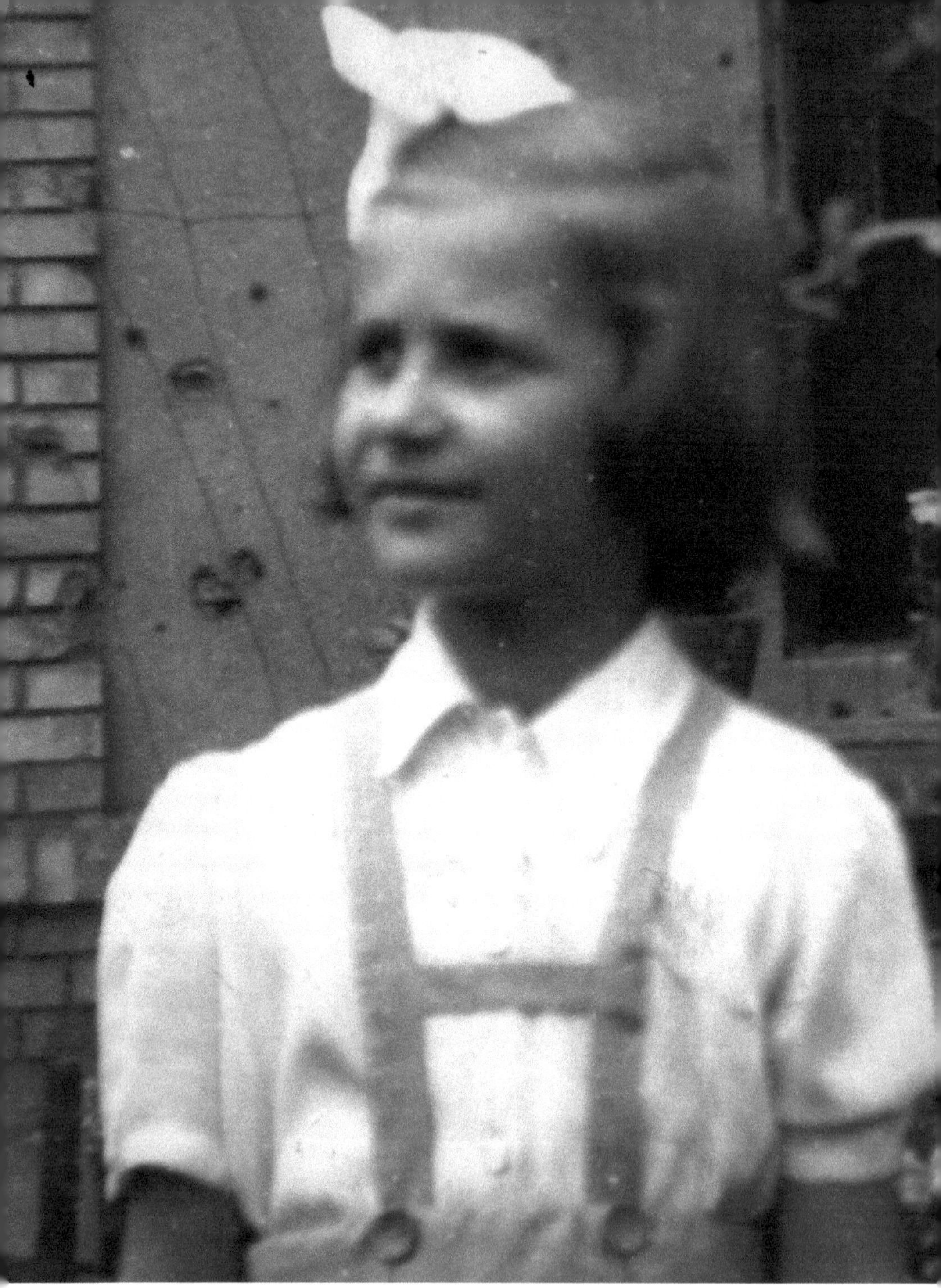

2.8. Contemplating leaving the country at the age of ten.
Source: Family Collection.

From the perspective of a young schoolgirl, my first thought when hearing about all the turmoil was: "Great! There won't be any school!"

And schools did, in fact, close. But then my parents began to show me what to do if I heard a siren.

"You dash down three flights of stairs and head straight to the basement. Do NOT use the elevator."

"Why not?"

"Because they may bomb the building."

And the sirens did sound, and we did have to shelter in the basement of the building. When they stopped, we headed back up the stairs, and my parents began to fill the bathtub and the sinks in case the water was shut off. This might be our only source of drinking and bathing water for days.

Life as we knew it was changing rapidly. Suddenly, we were not getting fresh food every day because my mother was not allowed to even leave the house. We were all in lockdown because of the riots and repression in the streets.

I remember one evening, having been cooped up in the house most of the day, my mother started feeling sick to her stomach. There was no way of running out for a doctor's appointment. There was not even a doctor's office open anywhere. Fortunately, a doctor lived in our building, two floors above us. My dad dashed up and asked him if he would come down to examine his wife. The physician determined that my mother had appendicitis and needed surgery immediately.

With the chaos and the violence in the streets, and the Molotov cocktails flying around, it was impossible to call an ambulance. Moreover, the young students had taken over the ambulances to transport guns and ammunition. As a matter of fact, we later learned that at least eight of every ten ambulances that drove that day had been blown up by the Soviets, who knew exactly what they were being used for.

Knowing this, what choice did we have? Either take an ambulance to the hospital and risk being targeted or die in the apartment.

By then, my mother was a physical and emotional wreck. She was in such bad shape that she had to be carried down the stairs to the front door to hopefully flag an ambulance. The only transportation allowed on the streets at this point were tanks, armoured trucks, ambulances, and police cars.

They managed to secure an ambulance and took their chances. Luckily, my mother made it to the hospital, and the surgery was successful. She went through the entire ordeal by herself, since no family members were allowed. With this kind of operation, the hospital usually kept a patient for three days to monitor their health, without any visit, but my mother returned home earlier than expected.

The doorbell rang and, as we opened the door, she collapsed into my father's arms. When she came around, we asked her why she had left on her own.

"What were you thinking? We thought you were in the hospital."

"I couldn't stay any longer."

"Why not?"

"Last night, the woman in the bed next to mine was shot dead by a stray bullet that came through the window."

The next morning, my mother had gotten up and dressed as quickly as she could. She made her way home, hugging the walls and ducking into alcoves, while ensuring the roads were safe.

* * *

The revolution was escalating. Hand grenades and other war materials had been added to the mix. For the next three or four nights, I could hear my parents talking a lot. I had no clue what was going on, but they were deciding whether to leave the country or not. They gave my sister and me the news the next morning. A whirlwind of questions went through my mind. Where are we going? What can we bring? How long will we be on this so-called holiday?

But this would not be a holiday. We were leaving forever. We could not take suitcases with us because we could not let anyone know we were escaping. We had to leave all our friends, family, and favourite things behind.

This was the most shocking part for me. To this day, every time I see someone's most precious and cherished belongings, I wonder if they would be able to leave it behind if told to. My favourite toy at the time was a doll carriage, a miniature version of the elaborate baby carriages they made in Europe back then, with a porcelain doll that had blinking eyes, eyelashes, and real hair. Even though I hardly played with them, they meant a lot to me. The morning my parents told me we were leaving, my father said I could only take one or the other. My first reaction was:

"If I can't take my carriage and my doll, I'm not going!"

It was hard enough that I could not let anybody know I was leaving. But not being able to take my favourite things along with me was simply unbearable. At that point, my father did something he had never done before. He slapped me across the face and said in a firm tone:

"Young lady, you will do as you are told!"

It is easy to imagine the state of mind my parents were in at that time. My mother had just come out of the hospital. The country was falling apart before their eyes. And they had just been faced with the toughest decision of their life. And now this little kid was fussing over her carriage and her doll. In the end, only my doll came with me.

By then, the situation in the streets had calmed down. A few weeks had passed, and people were beginning to go out at certain times of the day. My best friend Graci came over to pay me a surprise visit. She literally arrived right after the big slap. Checking myself in the mirror before opening the door, I saw that four or five fingerprints were still noticeable on my face. What was I to do? I could not have my girlfriend see me like that. I ran to the bathroom and put talcum powder all over my face. I looked like an absolute ghost. I opened the door and, naturally, she reacted:

"What happened to you?"

"My sister and I were playing, and I was pretending to be a ghost."

I had to hide the truth from her. I could not publicize that my family was about to leave Hungary. We would be sitting behind bars within the next hour, at most, once the news got out.

Fortunately, my friend found nothing amiss about my story. She walked into the house and said:

"How do you feel about no school for so long?"

"It was all right at first. But now, after weeks and weeks of it, I'm getting quite bored."

We chatted about the activities we had done over the period that we were forced to stay at home. After that, she said:

"I came over to borrow a couple of books from you."

I went to my little cabinet. She knew me well enough to know how much I loved all those books, notebooks, pads, pencils, and pens that I collected. When I opened the cabinet, I took everything that I had and gave it to her in one big heap.

"Georgia, I asked you for two books. What are you doing?"

"Take it. I want you to have them all."

"But those are your favourites! Why don't you want them?"

"I've outgrown them. I don't need them anymore. Take them; they're yours."

"You've got to be crazy," she responded, as she walked away with a whole bunch of books and stationery that she knew were very special and very dear to me.

I knew we were leaving the next morning and that I would never need those things again.

I had to detach myself. From my books, from my best friend, from my Budapest life.

3 Epic Escape: Fleeing from Tyranny (1956–1957)

WE SET OUT the next morning: my father, my mother, my sister, and myself. My sister was six years old, and I was ten. The only thing you could tell by looking at us was that something was up. If you looked more closely, you could notice that each one of us was wearing a double set of clothing. Two sets of long pants, two sets of sweaters, and an extra jacket for me and my sister. My father was wearing two suit jackets and two sets of suit pants. My mother, double sweaters, and double coats. Mind you, it was November by then, so it did not look completely ridiculous. All this, of course, because we could not be seen leaving carrying a suitcase. My mother did have some sort of basket with her.

In the morning, we left for the train station. Taking a car or a taxi was not a safe option. Trains still ran since they supplied the city with food, equipment, and medication. We had contacted an uncle who lived quite close to the border with Austria and who might possibly be able to help us cross. Looking back, it felt just like in the movies. We had an agreement with my grandparents, who stayed behind. If there was a problem, if we were held up, or if we were arrested by the police, we would call them. And if we made it safely across the Austrian border, then we would print a coded note in the newspaper that stated, "We no longer need fabric for the machine" (my grandmother was a seamstress, and they were interested in sewing machines).

This was the original plan. We arrived in Győr, the city near the Austrian border where our relatives lived. The people there had not experienced the same type of fighting as in Budapest. When my great uncle came to meet us at the train station, he took us to his home and told us, "I have bad news for you. The Russians are swarming the city. They arrived here just a week ago. I couldn't let you know on the telephone. Unfortunately, I cannot help you. I'm very sorry! You made the trip for nothing. We'll welcome you into our home and house you, but we can't help you beyond Győr as we had hoped. I do have a friend in another town who knows about you, however, and who would be willing to help. He can safely guide you and get you at least closer to the border."

We did not know this friend, we had no picture of him, and he did not know what we looked like.

"How will we find each other?" my parents asked.

"We've got that all arranged. Remember those hats, your father may still have some around, called fedoras? They have a ribbon the same colour as the hat. He will have a little piece of paper in the ribbon of his hat over his right ear. You [meaning my father] will do the same thing. When you get off the train, all you do is walk along the platform. When you see a man with a little piece of paper over his right ear only, under the ribbon of his hat, and he sees you with the same thing, that's your man."

This sounded like a wonderful plan. My sister and I were so excited! We got on the train and went to the little town, just an hour away or so. We got off and started looking around. Who would have the paper? The whole thing felt very adventurous to me. We eventually found the man. Unfortunately, it was the same story as in Győr. He told us that a few days ago he could have helped us out, but that it was no longer possible. The whole town was now under surveillance. My mother and father had lost all hope and figured that we may as well book a train back to Budapest. But our contact was more hopeful: "I have another idea. The Russians haven't positioned themselves in the villages yet. There's a farmer who's made himself a mint by guiding people like you across the border. Why don't you give that a try? I can tell you how to get there by train. At this point, what have you got to lose?"

He was right. We had tried twice already; we might as well do it a third time.

We got on a new train, this time heading to the countryside villages. The passengers were mostly farmers commuting back and forth to various farming jobs. On these old-fashioned trains, there were little open verandas or platforms between the train sections to go from one car to another, called *perrons* in French as well as in Hungarian. A group of around five farmers stood out there smoking their pipes and their cigarettes, talking on their way home from work. We found our seats and sat down quietly, trying not to draw attention to ourselves. As the farmers came back into the car, they looked at us and laughed:

"There's a bunch of people trying to escape!"

For our safety, secrecy was key. Yet here they were, yelling out that we were attempting to leave.

One of them even shouted:

"Hey man! Don't you like your home country anymore?"

They began heckling us. It is easy to imagine how nervous we already were without these farmers grilling us:

"Are you leaving the country? Is it not good for you here anymore? Are you not a patriot? What's going on with you?"

"No, no, we're just visiting friends," my father replied.

"Sure, you're visiting friends. It's written all over you. Do you always wear two suits when you visit? Do your kids get bundled up in extra clothing when you're visiting friends? Do you take us for fools? What are you trying to prove?"

How does one respond to that? Admit or deny? Were these farmers friends or enemies? We could not tell whose side they were on. That scared us even more.

Rather than risking a fistfight with these angry men and getting into more trouble than we already were, my father chose to come clean.

"Yes, we're planning to leave the country," he confessed.

Upon hearing this, one of the men launched into a long speech.

"We sympathize with your cause and understand how you are feeling. We only wish we could be doing the same thing as you, but we are not able to in the current circumstances. We are willing to offer you our help."

The man paused for a moment, gauging our reaction to this offer. Seemingly satisfied, he continued.

"The train conductor realizes there are people on board who wish to escape, and he's doing everything he can to help. The village this train is bound for was overtaken by the Soviets this morning. If you disembark station side, you will regret it, because you will run into a 'welcoming committee' of twenty to thirty Russian soldiers armed with machine guns, waiting and ready to arrest you. They will incarcerate you for months for trying to escape. However, there is another possibility."

Again, he paused, looking at us closely, before continuing in a low voice.

"It will be difficult in your case with two children, because it is a question of timing. When you arrive at this destination, the conductor will stop and let off extra steam. He'll let a lot out. At that moment, you jump off the other side of the train, on the field side, where there will be a big embankment. You will most likely fall and roll down. But if you manage not to get hurt and run to the nearest house and hide behind the fence before the train pulls out, then you will be safe. Good luck to you! That is all we can tell you because our stop is here. Remember, get off on the wrong side of the track!"

Wow, this was just like in the movies!

That was a lot of excitement and adventure for one little girl to take in a single day. When the train finally stopped and let out some steam, we took advantage of the noise and the smoke to get up and jump out on the opposite side. My father was there to reach up and assist my sister and me. As for my mother, who was fresh out of the hospital, he lowered her down and then held on to her. I can now sympathize with the pressure my father was under. He had to make sure all three of us got off safely at a moment when every second counted and could possibly mean the difference between life and death. We ran as quickly as we possibly could across the field, got to the house, rounded the corner of the fence, crouched down, and peered back to look at what we had just left behind. That scene has stayed in my mind's eye ever since. It is something that I will never forget. Other people like us, who did not have the good fortune of being warned, had disembarked onto the platform and were now being arrested at gunpoint by Soviet soldiers.

We did not stick around to observe how the scene unfolded. We immediately proceeded down the roadway to the farmhouse, where we were to meet the guide who was to help us cross into Austria. It was within sight, right after rounding the corner from the fence where we were hiding. The tiny old farmhouse consisted of a single room with dirt floors and a small fireplace. It was all very cold and damp. There was no bathroom inside and I needed to go after all the stress caused by our narrow escape from the Soviet soldiers. My only option was to run to the outhouse, some twenty yards away. This was new for me, and it made the little city girl, used to the comfort of her own home, nervous and afraid. I had to face this fear alone, since my parents, who were busy dealing with the farmer, could not accompany me. Once I got there, my imagination got the better of me, and I became convinced that the twenty soldiers from the train station were waiting outside with their guns. I was terrified, making it even more difficult to relieve myself. Of course, this was just all in my head. I eventually emerged from the outhouse, trembling from head to toe, and dashed back to the relative safety of the farmhouse.

Many people had already gathered there, waiting for the final group to arrive, which was us. We were fourteen adults and seven children in total. The farmer welcomed us.

"I'm the guide who will help you reach your destination. But I will do it for a price. What are you ready to pay me?"

My parents were in no position to fork out thousands of forints, the Hungarian currency. We only had a little bit of money, a few watches, and some jewelry, which we proceeded to hand over. These people did not have much. The payments they collected helped them build a small fortune. The farmer understood that most of us had not been able to bring money with us, so whatever valuables were to be had would do, whether rings, watches, jewels, or shoes. For those shoes he liked, he demanded that we take them off and, in exchange, put on his old muddy shoes in the cupboard.

Once the transactions were completed, the farmer agreed to take our group after nightfall. Since his fields extended over the border, he was very familiar with the terrain, and it was easy for him to show us the way to Austria. As we ran to freedom, I started to feel a very sharp pain in my side. I could not take another breath. I told my parents:

"I can't move. It hurts."

Well, you do not stop a group of people who are escaping because a little girl has a side stitch. Everybody just kept on running, and I just had to keep up.

I remember my mother sticking something in my mouth, maybe an aspirin, and just telling me:

"Come on, let's get moving."

We quickly arrived in the farmer's fields. Every two to three steps, we had to knock off the mud from our shoes. It was quite a cumbersome walk.

Over the course of what seemed like a never-ending trek, a flare suddenly shot up in the middle of the night. I was immediately shoved down face first into the thick, sticky mud. As a child, I did not understand what was happening, so I had to get an explanation.

"Why did you just push my face into the mud?"

The stranger who had dragged me down replied:

"Because if you were standing when those flares lit up, they would have shot at you."

"They" being the Soviets, of course, and the reason they were shooting those flares was to find anybody running across the fields and escaping from the country. If the light revealed silhouettes, they would open fire.

"So, if you see another flare going up, don't stop and look at how pretty it is. It will turn you into an easy target. Lay down on your face as fast and as flat as you can."

There were two more flares afterwards, and I did not stop to admire either of them.

We eventually reached the shore of a river. Our guide turned to us and said, "So long. I will not be able to take you any further. If I do, I risk my own life."

I suppose he was afraid because this had been the first morning the Soviets had come to his village.

"See that neon cross far, far away in the distance? That's an Austrian church. Good luck. May God bless you."

He was gone in an instant, leaving us alone in the dark. In all the excitement, we forgot to ask him how to cross the river. It was November and there were seven children in the group. Swimming across was too dangerous. What would we do?

In that moment of crisis, this group of strangers, who had never seen or talked to each other before that evening, became instant friends. We pooled our resources, working together and for each other, not only for ourselves. Two men decided to go in opposite directions. Fifteen minutes was the deadline. If neither of them found a bridge in that time, they were both to return. One of them returned after seven minutes; he had found a small and rickety wooden bridge. Once the other fellow returned, we successfully crossed the bridge and the field, guided by the neon cross.

My mother and I were the last ones walking in the group. She had just been through surgery, and her stamina was rapidly declining. She was not doing well. As a matter of fact, we were falling behind the others. My father was carrying my sister on his shoulders, and he was slightly ahead of us. At one point, my mother fell. Naturally, like a good daughter, I tried to encourage her and assist her.

3.1. Hungarian refugees quartered in a Siemens building in Wopfing, Austria, December 23, 1956.
Source: Family Collection.

"Come on, Mom, get up. I'll help you."

"No, no, no," she protested. "You go ahead with your father. I'll catch up."

Somehow, I was not convinced that she would follow if I went ahead. In that moment, I knew what I had to do.

"No, I'm not leaving you here alone. Dad is now about ten, twenty steps ahead."

It was pitch black and we could barely make out shapes. Mom was lying there, weak and tired, giving me no indication that she was going to be able to catch up very soon. I was not about to leave her or go anywhere. She begged me:

"Georgia, you have got to go. I don't want you to be in trouble. Move!"

"As soon as you come," I insisted, "I will go."

What I was not aware of at the time was that, when she fell, her boot got caught in a barbed wire fence. It was only many, many years later that my mother told me that this was one instance when, in a way, my disobedience and stubbornness had saved her because she was exhausted and had come to the end of her strength. But when she saw that I was not ready to catch up to my father and sister, and that giving up now would not only endanger her own life but also jeopardize mine, she pushed and pulled until she was finally able to free herself from the fence. Her boot still had barbed wire marks on it, but she got up and we managed to catch up with the rest of the group.

In fact, nobody had noticed we were missing. Since everybody was whispering to each other so as not to be detected, we could not shout: "Hey Dad, wait up, please!"

When my father understood what had happened, I remember him saying:

"I don't care what happens moving forward, but the first human being we encounter that's Austrian, I'm going to kiss them."

As we kept walking along, I got tired and miserable. A little boy about my age came up to me and started to walk beside me in friendly encouragement. When I fell a few times in the muddy areas, he grabbed my hand and continued to walk with me. He distracted me by talking with me about school.

As we neared the neon cross that had been our beacon in the night, this great, big, bearded farmer came towards us. He looked quite surprised to see a group of fourteen people come out of his farm field. As promised, my father ran right up to him and kissed him. And as soon as we explained our situation to him, where we came from and what was going on, the expression on his face quickly went from puzzled and concerned to understanding and empathetic.

"I know what you're talking about. A few weeks ago, we set up our church basement for people like yourselves. Let me bring you there and get you something to eat."

He took us to the church basement, which had mattresses set up and hot chocolate prepared for the children.

Back home in Budapest, one of the biggest presents I would receive at Christmas was an orange. Bananas, I did not even know until we came to Canada because my parents simply could not afford to buy us that kind of fruit. So, when the Austrians welcomed us with hot chocolate and chocolate bars, as kids we were delighted. We enthusiastically accepted everything they offered us and constantly asked for more.

* * *

Since my father and mother spoke quite a bit of German, they were able to communicate fairly easily with our hosts, who now explained that they would take us to some army barracks. There, we experienced what they now call communal living, with fifty people crammed in one room with bunk beds. That was how we lived for our first week in Austria. We were subsequently housed in a beautiful three-story building owned by the Siemens electrical company. This was a vacation resort for its employees and was vacant in the winter. I vividly remember the Christmas we spent there, the snow covering the ground. Every child got a sweatsuit, which was such a beautiful present. We were extremely grateful for these clothes because we had come with only two outfits, and after a while they had begun to wear thin.

It was at this time that our Austrian hosts began to ask us: "What is it that you want to do? Do you want to settle in Austria? Do you want to go elsewhere? What would you like to do with your future?"

My father had always hoped to go to Australia, if he ever had the money. We were then sent to Vienna to secure our tickets for Australia. There was a substantial lineup in the waiting room to get our flight tickets. Instead of sitting there, my dad decided to walk about to see if he could find us some small Christmas gifts. He had no money but decided to meet up with an old colleague who would lend him enough to buy my sister and me a little something. When he returned to the ticket office with all the candy he could afford, he was surprised to find that it was too late.

The doors had closed. And so, we never moved to Australia.

My parents sat down, hopeless.

"What will we do now?"

My father knew one man in Montreal. Not a close friend—a mere acquaintance. Based on this, my parents decided it would be best if we headed to Canada, where we would have a chance to benefit from this man's support, if needed.

And so, my father signed us up for Canada.

As I reflect on this pivotal moment, all I can think of was that this was truly a "sliding doors" moment, like the 1998 movie, which depicted two different life stories depending on whether the main character caught a train or not.

4 Arriving in Canada: New Life, New Culture (1957–1959)

After clearing and signing all the papers at the Canadian booking office, we were scheduled to leave on February 15, 1957. That was a special day. The Canadian military, which flew us to Canada, immediately made a strong impression on me, as did the kind and considerate attendants on board.

Naturally, I had never been on an airplane before, and I kept worrying that we would crash if one of the propellers stopped functioning. Our flight landed in Newfoundland, and I remember eating in the officer's mess that night. I also remember having a very sick stomach from eating far more than I needed to. I had put every little item of food on my tray that was available. They had, after all, told us to choose whatever we wanted to eat, and Mom and Dad could not prevent me from overindulging by saying, as they always did, that they had no money.

Not only did I develop a sick stomach after that time, but within days I got a high fever, which turned into the flu. My frail body was clearly not ready for the harsh Canadian February weather. So much cold and so much snow was hard to fathom for a young European girl.

After our stopover in Newfoundland, we were to stay in the barracks at Uplands Airport in Ottawa. But upon arrival, it was decided that this little kid was far too sick to stay. They rushed me to the hospital.

Imagine yourself in my shoes. I was a ten-year-old in a foreign land. A frozen country, with mountains of snow. I did not understand more than ten words of English. Back in Hungary, at the end of the school year, the teacher handed out an English storybook to everyone but me. I put my hand up and enquired:

"You forgot to give me a book."

The teacher responded with disdain.

"I did not forget. I wasn't going to give you a book because you don't know enough English to be able to read it. You will never learn to speak English."

How I would love to go back to that moment and tell her that I eventually became an English teacher.

Teachers should never try to predict the future of their students. No one has the power to know what the future holds for the students in our classrooms, however, challenged they might be as children.

But I am getting ahead of myself.

Back at the Civic Hospital, they tucked me into bed and gave me all kinds of tender, loving care. I had no complaints. But something bothered me: The other children all seemed to have beautiful slippers and warm, cozy pyjamas. I had neither. I had one of these horrible hospital gowns that tied together at the back and left everything "open to the world." The nurses very patiently explained, as best they could to a child who did not know the language, that the lovely sleepwear had been brought in by the mothers and fathers of each child. Their parents could afford these things, whereas mine could not. I felt "lesser"—less well dressed, less visited, less important. Simply less. My parents were not even able to visit me, since they were stuck at the airbase.

I felt abandoned and scared, and I could not communicate and explain myself to the nurses.

My family was still staying at the Uplands Airport barracks when I was released from the hospital, but the time had now come to find more permanent housing. Canada acted with extraordinary speed, care, and planning in its support of the 37,500 Hungarian refugees who arrived between 1956 and 1958. These fellow Hungarians chose Canada to escape persecution, flee brutal repression, and secure basic freedoms for themselves and for their children. For my parents specifically, it was to guarantee that my sister Kati and I would be able to study beyond Grade 8 and not be forced to work in a factory for the rest of our lives.

* * *

Canada offered a vast array of support services, both social and financial, while the pre-existing Hungarian-Canadian community, established in the country since the late nineteenth century, was actively involved in our resettlement. The diaspora was there for newcomers to Ottawa as well as for those going to Montreal, Toronto, the Prairies, or to Vancouver. These communities helped tremendously by collecting and distributing the necessities, finding housing and jobs, strengthening the cultural life of the refugees, and fostering a renewed sense of Hungarian heritage and pride. The Canadian government helped by simplifying immigration procedures and chartering over two hundred flights of refugees from Austria. It also covered refugees' travel costs and financially supported their resettlement for their first year in Canada.

In Ottawa, residents accommodated a total of four thousand refugees, putting them up until they were able to stand on their own two feet and support themselves. My family benefitted from a peculiar kind of placement. We happened to be placed with the American ambassador and his family, who agreed to house us until we were able to settle in Canada and manage our lives on our own. Their amazing residence was in the posh neighbourhood of Rockcliffe Park. As a child, I was obviously fascinated. I had never lived in a house like this in my entire life. They had a maid and all kinds of extra bathrooms.

They also had a personal chauffeur, with whom I happened to work with years later at Freiman's (later The Bay). When he recognized me, he exclaimed: "Have I got stories to tell you!"

He did not have to tell me anything because by then I was quite aware that the ambassador's wife had not hosted us out of the kindness of her heart. As the chauffeur hinted, she seemed more concerned about how she was perceived, about being praised for her generosity, and, above all, about showing off to her elite Rockcliffe friends. Our own personal experience and interactions with her had already confirmed that she was not nearly as nice and welcoming as she made herself out to be. One very vivid memory I have of her was how she monitored who took bananas by keeping the seal on them (they were sold wrapped in paper back then). She did the same with ice cream. I remember being impressed by the big bricks of ice cream sold in Canada, and the quantity of ice cream readily available in a single household. I could not believe it.

In Budapest, I only ever had one scoop a week, on the way home from gymnastics. This was always a big moment for me. We never kept it at home because we only had a small ice box.

I remember one night going to the ambassador's wife and trying to communicate to her using signs that I wanted some ice cream.

"I'm sorry, we don't have any ice cream at home."

About half an hour later, her daughter was sitting up in her bedroom with a great big bowl of ice cream in front of her. Just stuffing it in.

This incident proved to me once and for all that the ambassador's wife was not as kind as she pretended to be. And to this day, I always have two great bricks of ice cream in my freezer, even though I do not crave it or enjoy it as much as I used to, after gorging myself on it for years once we could afford it.

It is amazing what kinds of things we carry into adulthood, especially if it is associated with a childhood memory of hardship or privation.

Despite the ambassador's wife and the (lack of) ice cream, we were sincerely grateful to this family for putting a roof over our heads, feeding us, and giving my parents time to find employment. But my parents did not wish to stay in this situation for long; nobody likes to live on charity. My mother and father both had enough education to aspire to decent and respectable jobs. And so, my father went out looking for work.

***

4.1. In front of the Ottawa family apartment on Lambton Avenue after living at the US ambassador's home, 1957.
Source: Family Collection.

Reality was quite different from what he had hoped. When you do not speak the language, you are not that young anymore, and you have children, you cannot be choosy about jobs. You have to take what is available. For my father, this meant becoming a shoe shiner.

I remember walking past the store one day and seeing my father kneeling at someone's feet to polish their shoes. Even though I was not all that mature, I felt deeply humiliated. I was also ashamed of feeling humiliated, and these competing feelings were too much to bear. I began to cry. A realization then came over me:

"Is this what Dad has to do for me?" I asked my mother.

She nodded.

4.2. Sledding, even on small hills, Ottawa, 1957.
Source: Family Collection..

"That's pretty deep love," I responded, shame having been replaced by profound gratitude.

Meanwhile, my mother was out making sandwiches for a great, big company. She worked in the cafeteria, so hard that her hands became raw from all the mayonnaise and the vinegar that she was mixing into the sandwiches. Once again, I was impressed by how much she, as much as my father, was ready to sacrifice for the family. In Hungary, she had a job with high responsibilities as a major buyer for a well-known newspaper company. Yet in Canada, my parents had to accept modest employment so they could build a future for our family. In his later years, my father found two jobs to provide a little more for us, selling sewing machines

4.3. Skating with modern skates, Ottawa, 1958.
Source: Family Collection.

for the Singer Corporation, and working night shifts at R. L. Crain Corporation, supplying ink for their printing business.

I remember the very first apartment in Ottawa we were able to afford with the jobs my parents had. It was a basement apartment. In the spring, I watched worms crawling through the window slots and down the walls. Our first piece of furniture was a sofa donated to us, which came with its own mouse. A mouse with a house. Despite this unwelcome guest, we were very thankful for the chesterfield. The second donation was a table and four chairs, along with a tiny pot, a can opener, a can of Campbell's soup, and a spoon. In Hungary, we did

4.4. **Still very happy to have the doll.**
Source: Family Collection.

not even know canned soup existed. That may have been all we had for supper for the four of us, but it was our very first meal in our new apartment. As for sleeping arrangements, I remember that we all slept together crosswise on the only mattress we had. Despite all these challenges, there was light at the end of the tunnel.

My parents had jobs that did not pay very well and because of that, money was tight. Very quickly, I learned the value of money. One time a man came to sell us silverware polish for five dollars. I decided to buy his product and took the amount from my mother's purse without letting her know. Afterwards, I was very proud to tell her that I had helped a door-to-door salesman. I felt empathy for him trying to earn a living in such a way. My mother was not impressed.

"That's so nice of you, Georgia," she said. "You just spent our milk money. Now, we won't have milk for the rest of the month. What do you think we're going to use silver polish for when we don't even have enough utensils for the four of us?"

My good heart and my charitable nature had clouded my judgment. A lesson harshly learned.

* * *

During that first year, I felt lost and extremely different from the other kids my age, in part because my parents could not afford to buy me a very extensive wardrobe. I attended Catholic school and, on one occasion, we went to a church celebration, and a teacher put a Kleenex on my head. I thought: "What? Why? My nose is not up there and it's not even running. What's happening?"

At that time, women and girls were still supposed to cover their heads. I did not have a hat, so the teacher placed a tissue on my head. I definitely felt out of place. When October came around, I discovered a new celebration called Halloween, which involved dressing up and wearing costumes. At that time, Canadian families did not go out and buy expensive costumes. They were created and made at home. But we did not even have a bed sheet to cut out a ghost costume. When I went home and told my mother that both my sister and I were expected to create something for the next day, she came up with a doable and imaginative solution. She went to get a bag of popcorn and sewed popcorn kernels all over both the sweatsuits we had received in Austria for Christmas. We were now "The Popcorn Sisters." Maybe we should have started a rock band.

A few weeks later, around the beginning of December, I found my seven-year-old sister Kati crying in our shared bedroom. I asked her what was bothering her.

"We moved so far away from Budapest," she whimpered. "How will Mikulás [Saint Nicholas, the figure who inspired that of Santa Claus] and Jézuska [Baby Jesus] find me?"

I eased my sister's anguish by telling her that Mikulás knew the location of all children across the world, even if they had moved.

According to Hungarian custom, children place a pair of polished shoes by the door on the evening of December 5 and wake up the next morning (the feast of Saint Nicholas is on the following day, December 6) to find them filled with chocolates and cookies. On December 24, it is Baby Jesus's turn to share Christmas presents with us. I still fondly remember the Christmas tree lights lit with real candles, and my father taking us both out for a walk around the park until the roller shutters of our apartment window were raised halfway, which meant that

4.5. A wonderful birthday party with new friends and neighbours, Ottawa, 1958.
Source: Family Collection.

my mother had finished decorating and wrapping the gifts and that we could go back to the apartment to celebrate Christmas.

Curiously, we had little to no connection with the local Hungarian community. My parents, who wanted nothing more than to forget their traumatic past (it was forbidden to ever mention our Jewish origins, under any circumstances, for fear of being persecuted), always said we should live like Canadians and make Canadian friends. Two terrific girls I met during that first year in Grade 5, Colleen and Gail, helped me every step of the way as I struggled to learn English. I am grateful that both are still around and that we are still very close friends to this day. From the New Edinburgh area of Ottawa, we then moved to Wurtemburg Street on the Rideau River. While living there, I had a great group of friends who were into badminton, street hockey, broom ball, and even tackle football. One of those friends, who is still in my life, Jean-Marc, has become the professional photographer of prime ministers and leading political leaders of Canada. He was gracious enough to agree to take my portrait for the cover of this book.

From there we moved to Langevin Avenue in 1958. This was an important move because we invited my grandparents to join us in Canada that same year. My mother missed her parents very much, and with the threat of the Communist state seizing their apartment constantly hanging over their heads, my grandparents decided to leave while it was still possible. There was another affordable apartment nearby on Douglas Street; this is where my grandparents established their new home.

When they arrived, my parents were anxious to see whether the suitcases my grandparents brought contained any of the large number of clothes they had left behind. Unfortunately, that was not the case. Since my grandmother was a great cook, she chose to fill one of her suitcases with kitchenware. To my father's great dismay, his mother-in-law preferred to take with her a heavy and cumbersome meat grinder rather than some of his suits. Personally, I did not care much about the contents of their suitcases. I was just delighted to be with my grandparents again.

⋆⋆⋆

Thinking back on my schooling days, I distinctly remember what happened when there was a fire drill at my first school, Rockcliffe Park Public. Because I had just arrived and practically did not understand or speak any English, I did not follow the instructions when the alarm sounded. Instead of leaving the classroom like everyone else, I panicked and hid under the desk. Emotionally, I was transported right back to Budapest. Years later, I met that Grade 5 teacher and she told me she had gone home that night and found all the information and newspaper clippings that she could about the Hungarian Revolution. She thought:

"Poor child! So frightened when she hears a fire alarm and so traumatized that she hides under her desk."

She then tried to teach us a little bit about what was happening in Hungary at the time. Because of the language barrier, I did not understand that she was teaching about my homeland, but some of her history and geography lessons spoke about the conditions that I had experienced. She said it was one of her best teaching years because the students could directly identify with what went on, rather than hearing about a far-off, abstract place somewhere in Europe. The students were more involved in the learning because they had a fellow student in the classroom who had actually experienced the trials and horrors of the revolution.

Another incident that I recall in that Grade 5 class was a math lesson on measurement using the imperial system of feet and inches. Our homework was to find out how tall each student was. I remember going home and feeling proud that I could finally participate and complete an assignment for the first time. For me, "feet" naturally referred to the part of my anatomy. So, I took off one of my shoes and measured my height by moving it along my body from the base of my foot to the top of my head. According to my calculations, I was six feet tall. I could hardly wait for the next day's math class. When it came to my turn to share the answer about my height, I was so proud to tell them that I was six feet tall. The entire class roared, laughing. The teacher asked me to show everyone how I measured myself. I proceeded to take off one shoe and repeat my technique.

The classmates laughed even harder and louder at my demonstration. I was confused and shocked at their reaction to my creative problem-solving. This episode crushed what little self-confidence I had and pushed me to further retreat into my shell of isolation and non-participation.

It was now September 1959. I had finished Grades 5 and 6 at St. Aloysius School and had to transfer to St. Brigid's School for Grade 7. Today that school building is the headquarters of a well-known charitable organization that feeds and clothes the unhoused and the hungry. It is an appreciated community service known as the Shepherds of Good Hope. Later, as a young family, my husband and I volunteered to serve food at this location for a few years.

Like a Refugee
by Tom Petty

5

"And They Called It Puppy Love": My One and Only (1959–1967)

IT ALL STARTED back in 1959 in Lowertown, Ottawa, when I first met Alan in my Grade 7 class at St. Brigid's School. Although he was still quite young, Alan recalls having somewhat of a "bad boy" reputation with the neighbourhood girls at the time.

"Yes," he recalls, "I was very popular with the girls in the late 50s. I hung out with older boys, I enjoyed being an athlete, I could dance well, and I was always invited to parties."

What he looked forward to the most was meeting the new students at the beginning of the school year, especially the girls. This is how he remembers first seeing me:

"I'll never forget that moment when Georgia was introduced to the class after transferring from St. Aloysius School. It blew me away. None of the girls that I had known in Lowertown, even though they were very pretty, were as exotic as her. I still use that word because that was the way I saw her. I still remember what she was wearing the first time I saw her: a red jumper and a white turtleneck. I had never really seen anyone wear those kinds of clothes together. I remember telling myself: 'I'm going to marry that girl.'"

Gypsy Woman
by Brian Hyland

He quickly learned that I was a bit of a tomboy who loved playing dodgeball, basketball, and volleyball. These interests brought me close to boys. At first, I liked a classmate named Desi. But I was competing with a very popular girl, Charlotte, who was allowed to go to parties and stay out, while I had very strict parents who did not allow it. Because of that, I did not have much of Desi's attention. However, one day Charlotte came along and said:

"You know what, Georgia, you can have Desi all to yourself because I like Alan now."

5.1. Alan, the Lowertown "bad boy," Ottawa, 1958.
Source: Family Collection.

I already had an eye on Alan because he was smart, funny, and always carried his rosary, the same one that hangs over our kitchen sink to this day. My friends encouraged me to approach Alan.

"Are you going to take Charlotte's leftovers, or are you going to go ahead and see if you can get Alan?"

They dared me. So I began to pay much more attention to Alan.

Occasionally, I was allowed to go to afternoon parties—never at night—where we played Spin the Bottle and Post Office. Alan turned out to be a good kisser (clearly, he already had some experience). But there was more to his versatile personality than that. He was also an altar boy. I had a hard time concentrating on what was going on at mass when he was up there. Of course, being a good

5.2. Grade 8 St. Brigid's graduation with teacher, principal, and best friend Gail Larkin, Ottawa, 1959.
Source: Family Collection.

Catholic girl, I had to go to confession and could not avoid mentioning the kissing games. I recall telling the priest:

"I kissed a boy several times."

"Did you kiss him like you would kiss your mother and father?"

"Um, not really."

"Well then, you need to do penance."

And I was given quite a penance.

I was not really allowed to date Alan at all because of my very strict European upbringing. Having just moved to a new country, my parents were suspicious of this unfamiliar environment and were afraid of possible bad influences on their young daughter.

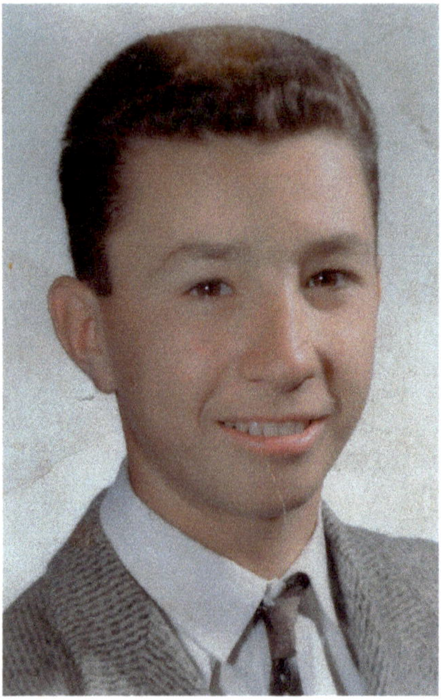

5.3. and 5.4. Alan and Georgia, both twelve years old, Ottawa, 1958.
Source: Family Collection.

"In Grades 7 and 8," Alan recalls, "we developed so many strategies to see each other secretly. It kept our minds busy and active, but it involved a lot of chasing around. How would we meet up or sneak out to a dance? Where would Georgia be with her family and how could I see her from a distance, hidden behind the trees at Rockcliffe Park?"

Oddly enough, despite the restrictions, Alan was allowed to come to our home to help me learn French. That was, after all, for academic purposes. He was a native French speaker, both his mother and grandmother were Franco-Ontarians from Ottawa. Like me, English was not his first language; he only began to learn it in elementary school.

"I wasn't just teaching the French language," Alan has always jokingly said. "I was also sharing French-Canadian culture by way of French-kissing."

I remember one time walking along Rideau Street and giving him a "lovey-dovey" look. My parents happened to drive by at that very moment. They immediately reacted, "For somebody who's merely teaching you French, you didn't look at him like he was just a study buddy."

I probably blushed and came up with some lame excuse, "Oh, but he said something so kind, and so nice, I just guess I had that look on my face."

We tried to keep everything secret as best as we could, but they were on to us. They once even asked me sarcastically: "So, you like that midget guy?"

5.5. Georgia at fourteen years old, Ottawa, 1960. *Source:* Family Collection..

That was because Alan was shorter than me at the time. Of course, he's now a full head taller than I am.

As with most teenagers, high school was a time of crisis and questioning, for us as individuals as well as for our relationship. Alan basically grew up without a father and looked up to the priests around him, many of whom had been athletes in their youth like him, as paternal figures and role models. Under their guidance, he considered entering the priesthood and at the end of Grade 8 joined the all-boys St. Pius X Minor Seminary on Fisher Avenue, in Ottawa. As for me, my parents, who were adamant about keeping me away from boys, decided to send me to a Catholic all-girls school, Immaculata High School. Throughout all this, we stayed together and continued dating, and our love continued to grow stronger. For five years, Alan kept a foot in each door—the secular and the religious—trying to figure out if what he really wanted was to be a religious Father or the father of a family. These were challenging times, since Alan could not make up his mind.

This major life decision loomed over our entire high school years and remained a major topic of discussion between us. It got to a point where my parents tried to get me to date other guys, to see if I was absolutely sure about my choice. I was not very enthusiastic about the idea, but I did agree to go out with one or two young fellows just to appease my parents. Alan, however, was not so appeased.

"When we were at dances and Georgia was with her date, I felt pretty jealous," Alan admits. "Fortunately, she was not overly interested in anybody else, which made me feel somewhat secure."

Throughout all this, I still could not understand how this smart, popular, athletic young man, who played football, basketball, and hockey, could be interested in a shy, introverted girl like me. A fun, outgoing, sociable guy, Alan had to drag

5.6. Georgia at nineteen years old, not in uniform, Ottawa, 1965.
Source: Family Collection.

me to high school dances. But I could feel I was important to him. One year I went to see Alan, who was the quarterback of his team, perform at the Pigskin Parade, a major city-wide event where all the Ottawa high school football teams paraded around Lansdowne Park before playing a short game. I could tell Alan was proud.

"I still treasure that moment," remembers Alan. "I felt like a hero, because it was something I could really do well. After the game, Georgia came up to me, and I tapped her on the top of the head. She was, after all, the most important person in my life. I was so grateful she was there, as my parents rarely showed up for my games. Georgia was always there for me. Her presence meant a lot to me."

⋆ ⋆ ⋆

I was so innocent back then. I would lick red Smarties to use as lipstick because I was not allowed to wear makeup. And the first time Alan kissed me, after chasing me around the New Edinburgh swimming pool, literally tackling me and sitting on me, I was petrified. Not because the kiss was not good, but because, in my mind and according to my upbringing, you could get pregnant from kissing.

One night, after helping me with my homework, my parents caught him kissing me on the forehead right before leaving. I was nineteen by then and I remember that my mother was shocked.

"What's going on with you two? He's kissing you now?"

As if that was a major kiss.

"You're getting upset about a forehead kiss?" I replied, insolently.

Now she was annoyed.

"What else are you not telling me?"

I got sassy.

"Well, if a forehead kiss gets you this excited and this upset, I think I'm just not going to tell you anything!"

* * *

I did not particularly enjoy my high school years. There were no boys, gym classes were lousy, we had to wear uniforms, and the nuns were always on our case about how sinful we looked when we were allowed to dress as we wanted.

Moreover, in Grade 12, I had to be rushed to the hospital to have my appendix removed.

Once I graduated, it was clear to me that I was done with school. I took a job with Metropolitan Life Insurance as a filing clerk. I had to sign an agreement that I was not taking this only as a summer job but as a year-long commitment. However, after two weeks of filing forms in alphabetical order, I knew I would never last an entire year. Fortunately, my boss was kind enough to hear my concern and said it might be a good idea to take a secretarial course at night, which would give me other options in the company. But I was not interested in that. After another month, I was very frustrated and again approached my boss. He asked me what I would do if he were to let me out of my commitment. "Become a teacher," I responded. I wonder if that response was because of my Grade 2 experience when, as a little girl, I was appointed to be the supply teacher when our teacher and the supply teacher both called in sick.

You know the saying, "The squeaky wheel gets the oil?" I am ever so happy I squeaked.

Apparently, a few weeks in an office was all I needed to realize how much I liked being in a classroom. I was accepted at Ottawa Teachers' College for a two-year program and went on to teach for eighteen years. I am still grateful to that boss for letting me out of my commitment.

5.7. Georgia at twenty years old, at Teachers' College, Ottawa, 1966.
Source: Family Collection.

When I graduated in 1966, the organizing professor asked me to give the valedictorian speech. I was shocked. I was still very withdrawn and lacked confidence at the time.

Additionally, I knew that Prime Minister John Diefenbaker would be there as a guest of honour.

"Why are you asking me?" I blurted out. "I'm not popular, I'm not outgoing, I'm a very shy and quiet student."

5.8. and 5.9. Georgia and Alan ready for Teachers' College graduation, Ottawa, 1966. *Source*: Family Collection.

The professor stated his case:

"But you're sincere, you're kind, you're aware, you know how to touch the hearts of people with what you have to say."

Wow! That was the first time that any adult had ever given me such a compliment. I was honoured and overjoyed, but also scared at the same time.

5.10. Alan's graduation and dinner dance with his fiancée, Ottawa, 1968.
Source: Family Collection.

After Teachers' College, I went for my job interview and I remember wearing my ruby birthstone ring, which I had received from my parents for my eighteenth birthday. One member of the interview committee looked at my hand and asked:

"What's that ring? Are you engaged? Because if you are engaged, we don't want you."

I was puzzled by such a severe comment. The interviewer continued:

"The next thing you know, you'll get married, get pregnant, and then we'll lose you. So. What's that ring all about?"

I recall being annoyed by the inferences they were making and abruptly responded:

5.11. Alan at graduation.
Source: Family Collection.

"It's my parents' gift to me for my eighteenth birthday. It has no connection to your concerns."

I ended up getting hired.

I have always loved my teaching career and never really experienced discipline problems. When there was a challenge with a student, I would simply ask:

"Do you want to stay in detention, or can you cut out this behaviour?"

This usually puts an end to any nonsense. I have always felt, and Alan has shared this philosophy, that children have the same rights and feelings as adults. In my long experience, I have found that such a respectful approach and method of relating to students ultimately pays off in spades and is returned hundredfold.

* * *

In 1967, Alan completed his degree at Saint Patrick's College. He had finally decided which kind of father he wanted to be, and the priesthood was not for him. As my twenty-first birthday approached, he finally mustered up the courage to propose.

"I asked Georgia if she was interested in getting a paint job for her car?" After pondering the idea, she said: "No thanks; the car still looks fine." "Would you prefer a radio instead?" Again, after careful consideration, she declined. Once my practical offers had been denied, I went for a more romantic proposition. "What about if I propose to you and get you a diamond ring?" "Yes! Let's do it!" she screamed with joy.

I still break out in laughter when I recall this romantic proposal. To this day, I have never regretted accepting it.

5.12. Alan at graduation.
Source: Family Collection.

6

Family Life: Joyful Beginnings and Tragic Ends (1968–1976)

OUR ENGAGEMENT DEFINITELY did not resemble the type of grandiose proposals you hear about in the news today (at concerts, sports facilities, or even on airplane banners). Alan dealt with important situations in a straightforward and practical way. We both laughed about the way he proposed then, and we are still laughing about it now.

This was the beginning of our path to marriage, and it was there that we agreed to marry on June 29, 1968.

Why this specific date?

Because Alan's teachers' college training was set to begin after Labour Day weekend in Kingston, Ontario.

The wedding itself was not a huge, elaborate event. As a matter of fact, we only invited seventy-five people and the whole thing cost us $400 in total, the same price as my car. At the time I was making $3,200 a year.

The destination for our honeymoon was not an exotic place like the Caribbean. We went to Gananoque in the Thousand Islands region, on our way to Kingston. We picked the first motel we could find and did not even bother to get the wedding suite. We did not care either that our room was beside the owner's office. And what a lovely honeymoon meal we had the first night! Warm milk and cold smoked meat sandwiches, I will never forget it. Alan sure knew how to impress a girl...

As I write these memoirs, I realize that, after fifty-eight years of marriage, he still owes me an official honeymoon. Kidding aside, I never had high expectations for our honeymoon or for any trip—then, or now. To this day, I am easily pleased.

For the next two summers, we rented a cottage in the town of Godfrey, just north of Kingston.

Dream Come True
by Frozen Ghost

6.1. Wedding, June 29, 1968.
Source: Family Collection.

Mr. and Mrs. Imre Feuerstein
request the honour of your presence
at the marriage of their daughter
Georgia Mary Ann
to
Mr. Alan Richard Morissette
on Saturday twenty-nineth day of June
nineteen hundred and sixty-eight at eleven thirty a.m.
Our Lady of Mount Carmel Church,
400 St. Laurent Blvd.

Reception: Eastview Hotel R.s.v.p.

Figure 6.2. Wedding invitation, June 29, 1968.
Source: Family Collection..

When we were married, I had already been teaching grade school for two years. Alan had always wanted to be a teacher and a coach for students, but for him to become a high school teacher, he had to go to MacArthur College, which was Queen's University Faculty of Education. In the late 1960s, educators were badly needed to teach in the many schools being built to welcome the families of baby boomers. To fill these positions quickly, the Board of Education decided to include only two summers for the Teacher Education program.

Fortunately, because he was known in the city of Ottawa for his football skills, the principal of Saint Patrick's High School called Alan up and gave him a job. He was primarily hired as a French teacher but, because he was a rookie teacher, he was also given other subjects to fill his schedule, such as Latin, religion, and business education.

Perfect
by Ed Sheeran

WELCOME TO
MIAMI BEACH

6.3., 6.4., 6.5., 6.6., and 6.7. The "delayed honeymoon" in Miami Beach, Christmas, 1968, and New Year's, 1969.
Source: Family Collection.

On our first Christmas together, we went to Miami Beach, Florida with another couple who were teachers as well. I remember we went into a restaurant called Whopper King. We were the only Caucasians in the restaurant. All the other customers were Black.

This was 1968, and we had been following the Civil Rights Movement.

I remember asking the fellow in front of us in the lineup:

"Are you sure it's OK for us to be in here?"

"Oh yeah! Food is food for everybody! Enjoy!"

One of the interesting aspects of our first years of marriage was Alan's relationship with my mother Nadinia. One day, before we had children, she pulled him aside:

"You know Alan, you come from French-Canadian culture, and my daughter is a very fragile girl. She can't have ten, twelve, or thirteen children."

"That's fine with me! I am not necessarily interested in having twelve or thirteen children either," he coolly responded.

Alan kept that discussion always in the back of his mind. After all, he thought, Georgia's mother is just trying to protect her daughter in this new country with its very different traditions and customs. Because of my strict upbringing, I was still a virgin when we got married. The words of the song "*Wasted Days and Wasted Nights*," co-written by Freddy Fender back in 1959 and revived in 1980, come to mind whenever I think back to this moment.

Wasted Days and Wasted Nights
by Freddy Fender

6.8. Croatian beach with two-year-old son, Chad, 1973.
Source: Family Collection.

After three years, we decided to have children. We were both very curious as to what we could co-create and as to what these children might look like.

Our oldest son, Chad, was born in 1971, and our fraternal twins, Wade and Alanis, in 1974.

When our first son was two, the three of us took a trip to Hungary and Austria. In Austria, we visited the Siemens employee vacation complex in Wopfing, where my family and I were first sheltered as refugees in 1956.

Some of my relatives still lived in Budapest in 1973. They were so thrilled to see us, they booked the entire day with us starting at 7:30 a.m. We were incredibly touched, but that was not exactly our idea of a vacation! So, we took it upon ourselves to get out of town and escape just the three of us to Dubrovnik, Croatia (then Yugoslavia) to spend some extra holidays there.

We thoroughly enjoyed our time together with our little Chad, the leisurely pace, the incredible beaches, the wonderful food, the rooftop restaurants, as well as the hospitality of our Croatian hosts. When we arrived, we knocked on doors to see who might put us up because the hotels were way too expensive for our budget. We eventually found a place with a very welcoming Croatian family who lived very close to the exclusive Hotel Excelsior. They even invited us to share their meals. That was our first experience combining French fries with slivovitz, a Balkan plum brandy.

We were very fortunate and very happy to welcome our unexpected fraternal twins in 1974. This came as a complete surprise to us—there were no ultrasounds at the time. I was two weeks away from my due date for our "second child" when I went to see the doctor.

"I seem to feel a head up here, right above the belly button," he observed. "You might have a breech birth. Let's have you go down for an X-ray."

After the X-ray, I asked the nurse if I could have a look at the results. I just wanted to know where that little head was. Sure enough, there was a head in the proper position. Happy about what I had seen, I went back upstairs thinking everything was fine until the nurse looked at me with a big grin on her face.

"What's happening?"

"Oh! I can't tell you, Georgia! That will be the doctor's job."

"I've been coming in here for nine months, surely you can tell me what put that grin on your face."

"OK, but don't tell the doctor I shared this information with you. You're going to have twins!"

When the doctor walked in, my mouth was still wide open. I was in shock! Yes, we were going to have twins. I could not believe it.

When we returned home after the birth, our dear three-year-old son saw us with two babies and reacted with great surprise:

"You had two babies? Like your two eyes? Where are you going to put them?"

"I am not sure yet myself, but for now they will both fit into the crib," I answered hesitantly.

Ever the teaser, Alan took this opportunity to revisit his earlier conversation with his mother-in-law.

"Remember, Mother, when we had that discussion about the fragility of your daughter and us not having too many children? Well, it seems she was able to handle having twins. I only wanted to have children one at a time, not in bunches."

Alan used to kid my mom all the time about that; over time, Nadinia came to laugh about it as well.

Since maternity leaves had not yet been negotiated into teaching contracts, I had to return to work in September, barely three months after the twins were born. With me having to go back to school, our challenge was to arrange childcare

6.9. The twins come home, Ottawa, June 1974.
Source: Family Collection.

for September. Our eldest was cared for by a lady close to my school who agreed to take on our twins too. When I showed up with a playpen a week before school started, she answered the door.

"Having thought over what we discussed, I came to the conclusion that it would be too much and too challenging for me to take care of your three children at the same time. Unfortunately, I won't be able to help you out."

I was devastated.

What was I to do? Fortunately, I have always believed in responding, not reacting, because my reaction in that moment would not have been the most measured... or the most polite. Still, I voiced my frustration:

"You were aware they were twins and that it meant two additional babies on top of our three-year-old?"

"I was so happy to have your son for the past few years, and so I was excited to have his siblings. Then I thought that it was way too much for me to handle."

I walked back to my car, distraught.

That eventually faded, and we moved into action mode. We decided to seek out a live-in nanny, and fortunately, we found one who turned out to be ideal.

She was with us until Christmas. In my conversations with her, I learned that she really was hoping to be a teacher, for which she was certified in Jamaica. I encouraged her to follow her dream. She eventually found employment, and while we were delighted for her, this also meant we had to once again find another nanny.

But I am getting ahead of myself.

With the summer over, it was now September 3, 1974. As I returned to work on the first day of school, with barely three months of experience as a mother of three and a last-minute childcare solution, I felt very anxious to face new students, new staff, and new challenges.

When I came home from school, exhausted but satisfied, I was pleased to see Alan waiting for me in the driveway of our three-bedroom bungalow on Kitchener Avenue. But he was not there to welcome me.

A tragic event had occurred during the day: a catastrophic car accident involving my father, my mother, and my grandmother on their way home from a routine doctor's appointment.

The news was devastating.

The faulty and bare-threaded tires on my father's Volkswagen Beetle caused him to hydroplane over the median on the Queensway, crashing head-on into another car going in the opposite direction. My father and grandmother were thrown out of the car and killed on impact. My mother, who sat in the back so that it would be easier for her own mother to get into the front seat, was seriously injured but survived the accident.

We went to the morgue to identify the bodies, and then to the hospital to see my mother. My entire body was shaking, and it took me a long time to be able to sit still again.

In the following weeks, I returned to teaching and made myself extra busy by taking a psychology course on Tuesday nights. This was my way of grieving and coping with the loss. On my way home from those classes, I would always drive past the scene of the horrific family tragedy at the Metcalfe exit of the Queensway. The tears that invariably ran down my face helped release some of the pain.

After a public inquest, it was decided that the median barrier on the entire Queensway would be raised and reinforced so that no car would ever again cross the barrier if it aquaplaned. Volkswagen was also made aware of this incident so

6.10. Fatal car accident on the Queensway, September 3, 1974.
Source: City of Ottawa Archives, MG011-10-4-J1686-2-1.

6.11. Father and grandmother's funeral, 1974.
Source: Family Collection.

that upon selling a car, the tire inspection became part of the regular maintenance with all dealerships.

After the tragic deaths, my mother Nadinia lived alone in her house for a year and then moved into a rental condo. We visited her regularly. Seeing her three grandchildren was always an enjoyable and uplifting experience for her. She always tried to find the good in any situation, no matter how dire. One day, she sat down with me. “You know, I’ve been racking my brain as to what the gift was in all this happening with the car accident. Both your father and your grandmother spoke poor English. They never wanted to go to a senior residence where they would feel so lost. I suppose the gift is they never had to.”

I found this answer difficult to accept as a blessing. But I eventually came to understand its meaning.

⋆ ⋆ ⋆

My life continued, busier than ever, occupied with the daily duties and responsibilities related to teaching, parenting, and marriage. During those years, my authentic self remained subdued and hamstrung by the tragic deaths and the dedication to a young family and career. I felt overwhelmed by all the expectations I had to meet or live up to. That was a lot of weight on my (still) frail shoulders. All this left very little time for myself and for my friends, much less to give a helping hand to others beyond my immediate family. I had forgotten who I was, and it never crossed my mind at the time to try to reconnect with my authentic bubbly self, which I seemed to have left behind when we fled Hungary.

One of the most striking insights I had during this period was realizing that, for decades, other people had been speaking for me and answering on my behalf, whether at home, at school, at work, or in social situations. After all these years, I was still reluctant to participate in discussions, I still felt self-conscious at social events, and was like a wallflower at parties.

Why could I not speak up for myself and find my own voice?

The next period in my life would see me come out of my shell.

Get Down On It
by Kool & The Gang

7 Move to Europe: The Rediscovery of My Authentic Self (1977–1980)

A NEW ADVENTURE for our family began when my maid of honour, Mary Ann, and her husband Vaughn, who was in the military, paid us a surprise visit. They called us asking for a somewhat urgent favour before returning to Germany, where he was stationed.

"Georgia! My husband is going to be in trouble because his hair is too long and we're flying back later this evening. Is there any chance you might be able to give him a haircut?"

I agreed, of course, and, as I was cutting Vaughn's hair, they began to talk about how wonderful it was to live in Europe. They mentioned how much fun they were having, and how we should go ahead and join them by applying to go teach in Europe. They would welcome us and show us around.

Soon after they left for Germany, we both applied for a teaching position in Lahr, West Germany. Alan was already on board because he was always studying world geography. He had been reading about beer festivals in Germany in the *National Geographic* magazine, and specifically, the Hofbräuhaus festival in Munich.

This was initially a two-year loan of service agreement. It provided continuing tenure with our school boards and would be considered part of our teaching years, even though we were out of the country. Alan was vice principal at a junior high school at the time, and I was happily teaching Grade 5. Alan's job offer was to teach French and mine was to teach Grade 7, which was out of my comfort zone.

Such a leap of faith was a major decision for us to make. Leaving my still grieving mother behind was extremely difficult and heartbreaking, yet I knew my dear sister Kati was equally caring and would take good care of her. This was an opportunity I knew we could not pass up. I have always been a strong believer in staying open to new and adventurous possibilities in life.

This decision also responded to a deep-seated desire I always felt to return to my European roots, which had been "robbed" from me in my childhood. At the

7.1. and 7.2. Our Volkswagen camper van, Heiligenzell, Germany, 1977–1978.
Source: Family Collection.

airport when we left, I was the only wife not crying; I think that spoke to my confidence about beginning a new life.

When we landed in Lahr, West Germany, we were met by our sponsors, who would set us up and help us settle in. Our sponsor happened to be our principal Ken Culham, who is still a dear friend to this day. In fact, his eldest son Cam Culham was our best babysitter during those years in Lahr.

We were housed in a three-bedroom apartment in a village called Heiligenzell, which became our home for the next three years. Each of our three children got a room. Our eldest son, Chad, was six years old, and Wade and Alanis were three. We set up our bedroom in the living room. Our bed stood on bricks and there was a TV that only played German commercials. Even though we had no telephone, no newspaper, and no radio, we were still very happy to adjust to our new lodging.

We enrolled the children in school. Chad was in Grade 1 at the Canadian French Immersion school, while Alanis and Wade went to a German *Kinderschule*

for three-year-olds. Interestingly, the German kindergarten was a whole day program until 5:00 p.m., with two hours between 11:00 a.m. and 1:00 p.m. for lunch. Thinking back to our Canadian experience, we felt that this was rather a long day for two toddlers. The fact that they did not speak the language was a further challenge for them. A German neighbour of ours was responsible for taking them to school and picking them up. Eventually they began to speak German, especially when they did not want us to understand what they were saying. Mischief was already brewing with our wonderful Gemini twins.

***

In the intermediate school, Grades 5 to 7 were on the main floor. Always connected, Alan and I were assigned to adjoining classrooms. This was a good thing, not only because we enjoyed each other's company, but also because I needed extra space for the teaching tools that I wanted to include in my class. This meant that I could borrow some of Alan's cabinets for my teaching material. One time

7.3. and 7.4. Our Chrysler station wagon and a German caravan camper, Heiligenzell, Germany, 1979.
Source: Family Collection.

I needed to grab something from his cupboard, so I knocked on his door and entered. As I walked into his classroom, there was Alan standing on the window-sill. He was teaching the words "inside" and "outside" in French with one arm in the classroom and the other jutting out the window. I held my breath, waiting for him to possibly jump, simply to explain the two words. Perhaps it was not such a good idea for me to just come in unannounced when he was up to his demonstrative style of teaching!

One of the best things about Europe is that we were able to travel practically every weekend. We would visit amazing new places, new countries, and new landscapes, from the Swiss Alps to the great capitals of Berlin, Amsterdam, London, Dublin, and Rome. Luckily, we had brought over our Volkswagen camper van, which was always ready and packed up by Thursday night, as we would leave right after school on Fridays. On the way home on Sunday nights, we would consistently stop at German *Gasthofs* (restaurants) for our usual wiener schnitzels. In the

summer of 1978, we invited my mother to travel with us. One of the highlights of that vacation was a trip to the Greek island of Sifnos.

When we arrived on the island, we found out that there were no accommodations available. It was not our style to book ahead at that time. We were free-spirited. We also learned that the only bus to the next town, Apollonia, had already left. We decided to hitchhike but could not have everyone standing in the street with their thumbs out.

So, we used our Canadian experience, and everyone voted for me to be the only visible female blonde hitchhiker.

We knew already that only one car had come across on the ferry. And everyone had to take that same road to get to the town. So, I stood alone on the road hitchhiking while the rest of the family hid out of sight. That one car arrived hoping to pick only me up. It was then that the horde came out of hiding, and the poor driver was overwhelmed with fitting everyone into the car to go into town. The driver, George (it seemed all the Greek men were named George), became one of our best friends over the years and we wrote to each other when we returned to Canada.

One day, as we headed down to the beach, we saw beautiful yachts with naked people on board. My mother was not expecting this type of scenery and almost lost her balance on the stairs.

Since we were staying in very rustic accommodations, we had to wash either at a hand pump well on the street corner, or at the beach. One day, Alan managed to find an area where he could shower. He was very excited to finally be able to take a real shower.

As he went down to the walled building, he did not realize that it would be a free-standing outdoor shower on the beach. He saw a woman going to use one, so he went in on the other side, figuring that there was a partition between the men's and the women's showers. But to his great surprise, there was no such separation! We all wondered why Alan was taking so long. When he came back, he told us he had found himself naked with a bunch of Swedish ladies, assuring us that he had been a perfect gentleman and shared his soap with them. That evening, Alan met the same ladies at the restaurant where we were having dinner and started talking to them as if they were close acquaintances. Which I guess they were, in more ways than one!

* * *

In our second teaching year, one of my challenges was teaching music. Even though I have a nice voice, I have not always been very good at carrying a tune. So I would put on the *Sound of Music* album, and we would learn every word, song by song.

Suddenly, a light went off in my head: Why not visit Salzburg, where the *Sound of Music* was filmed?

I went to see my principal to ask if we could possibly get a school bus to take us to Salzburg for a few days. Knowing we had already used up the allotted travel money, I remembered my favourite adage: If at first you do not succeed, try and try again. So, I brainstormed ideas with the class. I asked the principal whether we could ask parents to drive to Austria. By then he was quite used to me thinking outside of the box. He agreed. Next, we raised funds to ensure that every student could go. For two months, the students took on chores and jobs to fund the trip.

Alan and I were going to take our camper. However, we thought it would be nice to have somebody help us out with our three children, who were also going to come along. As luck would have it, one of the girls in my class could not afford to pay her share of the expenses and risked not being able to join us on the trip. Would she consider helping to babysit our children and, in return, we would pay her fee? Such a big smile lit up her face!

We stayed in a dormitory in Salzburg, walked in the footsteps of Christopher Plummer, Julie Andrews, and the von Trapp family, and visited many of the beautiful movie locations, which created lasting memories for us. I am still in touch to this day with some of these students, who have told me that this particular field trip has remained a treasured memory of their European experience.

We made several interesting trips in our first two years in Germany. One of the most memorable ones was travelling with my mother, sister, brother-in-law, and nephew along with our children to Budapest in the summer of 1979. On several occasions prior to this trip, Alan and I had tried to obtain a visa to go to Hungary.

We were denied three times because we had a military stamp in our passports. As a matter of fact, we had to go to a remote, faraway entry point to cross the Iron Curtain. We were very fortunate that border crossings were not connected technologically back then. At last, we were able to meet up with the rest of the family, who had flown in directly from Canada, to share a heartwarming, rewarding experience.

We were all reunited in our homeland.

We visited our old Szent István Park apartment, where my mother's best friend, who also happened to be my sister's godmother, now lived. We were even followed several times by a black Mercedes, probably the Hungarian police, who wanted to keep an eye on this suspicious group of exiles. This brought back many difficult memories, both for my mother and myself.

We worried about getting out of the country, but everyone made it back home safely.

* * *

We now must go back to the early months of 1979 to explain how we were able to extend our loan of service for another year.

One day we were shopping for a German kitchen clock in the Lahr exchange store when we happened to bump into our educational superintendent.

"Oh, so you're going home?" he remarked.

"Yes, we are, although it's going to be hard because we love it here."

"Well, why don't you just stay another year?"

It was then, as we purchased the cuckoo clock, that we decided to seriously consider staying for a third year. The Ottawa School Board was putting a bit of pressure on Alan, as the school superintendents wanted to promote him to a position of principal upon his return to Canada. However, Alan and I felt so comfortable in Europe, and we enjoyed our lives in Lahr so much that we thought an extra year would be a more exciting and educational option for our entire family than returning home.

In truth, deciding to extend for a third year of magical experiences was very easy for us.

It was during this third year that a major event occurred.

The magnitude of this tipping point greatly impacted both my life and my personality, sparking me to rediscover my authentic self in every way.

In Germany, we did not have much in the way of home entertainment and we were rarely home on weekends. When we did not travel, the highlight for us was to go out to the officer's mess for weekly social events and meals on Friday evenings. Every time, a friend named Gail would come over to our table to greet us, chitchat for a bit, and then go on to her group to enjoy her evening. Once, she came up to me and abruptly said:

7.5. The German kitchen clock we brought home.
Source: Family Collection.

"Georgia, I have come here several times to greet you and share a conversation. Not once have you gotten off your backside to greet me when you had the chance. Is there some reason you don't initiate contact?"

I was baffled.

"What do you want me to say? Do I come to see you when I'm ready to leave, or when I have to go to the bathroom, or when I'm going to go get a drink?"

Her response was equally blunt:

"How about coming over to my table and asking how my week went. Then, when you want to leave, simply say: 'It was nice to see you! Enjoy the rest of your evening!' Do you think you can do that?"

"I believe I can!"

"Then next week, get off your ass and come visit my table!"

Believe it or not, that one conversation singlehandedly pushed me to revert to my authentic, extraverted self. You never know how you can influence someone by offering a single direct comment. I would like to thank Gail for teaching me about social interactions. What she said that night propelled me into re-establishing my true sociable and extraverted self, which had been repressed for so many years as a refugee.

7.6. German *Fasching* (carnival), 1979.
Source: Family Collection.

7.7. Medieval dinner with steel knives, 1980.
Source: Family Collection.

7.8. *Fasching* held in February each year before Lent.
Source: Family Collection.

Even after two decades in Canada, I still had the mentality and the instinct of an immigrant. I would keep to myself and only felt comfortable in a family environment or with a small circle of close friends. I was still very self-conscious about my accent and my mistakes in English, which made me hesitant and reticent to speak up or interact in public. All these fears and complexes disappeared when I returned from Europe.

⋆⋆⋆

It was customary for all teaching personnel to be given a flight back to Canada at the end of their stay in Europe. However, the military would only offer two tickets during the summer months, one for Alan and the other for me. We eventually found out that if the children flew before July, they could have their flights paid for. When we went to investigate this option, we met someone employed by the military who was taking a flight back two weeks before us.

7.9. Family skiing in the Alps.
Source: Family Collection.

7.10. Family skiing in the Alps, Berchtesgaden, Germany, 1979.
Source: Family Collection.

We asked him if he would consider escorting our three children back to the Trenton base, where our family would be there to pick them up and take them to Ottawa. He kindly agreed and asked if, in return, he could be driven back to Ottawa. We had him over for dinner so that he could meet the children and they would be comfortable with him while travelling. It was a win-win situation for everyone. Everything worked out beautifully. Thinking back on this, and given our children's ages at the time, I realize that very few parents today would feel comfortable doing what we did. Of course, times were different, and it was perhaps easier to trust a military member, but it was also a conscious decision on our part, a parenting choice we made, to teach our children to be comfortable around adults other than their parents, and to adapt to situations outside of their comfort zone, even at a fairly young age.

At the end of every school year, there was a big farewell ceremony for those teachers leaving Europe and returning to Canada. For our last year, Alan was

7.11. Teachers from across Canada.
Source: Family Collection..

selected to cohost the big event. In choosing a theme song, he picked one from Jimmy Buffett entitled, "*Changes in Latitudes, Changes in Attitudes.*"

Changes in Latitudes,
Changes in Attitudes
by Jimmy Buffet

It was a party of mixed emotions, and we all used to kid around with those leaving that they would be remembered as what's-her-name or what's-his-name. In fact, the opposite occurred. Throughout this wonderful experience, we made many lifelong friends among our fellow teachers and former students. To this day, students I taught in Germany still come over to our house for meals, go on double dates or even on holidays with us. This past summer, one of them even invited us to her daughter's wedding.

8

Parenting Beyond the Spotlight: Chad, Wade, and Alanis

I HAVE ALWAYS felt that, as both teachers and parents, Alan and I were always fairly unconventional, both in our style as well as in our methods—even for the times (in the 1970s and 1980s). We based our relationship with our children on trust and communication, just as we did with our students. These foundational values gave them the confidence to pursue their dreams, however big and crazy they might seem, knowing that we would always support them and be there for them. It is beautiful to see that we have been lucky enough to establish a similar kind of relationship with our grandchildren.

It all started with what we called "happy circles," a tradition that created a wonderful connection between parents and children while making the children feel comfortable to say whatever was on their mind. Today, we would call it a safe space. I remember, for instance, one time I found a lunch bag on the floor in the back of a toilet bowl and asked the kids who deposited it here. It was our older son; he said, "I didn't want to eat that, but I didn't want to throw it out." I said, "Guess what? Here are the four food groups that should be included in your lunches. You can make your own lunch from now on and choose what you wish to eat." This was not a punishment, but a way to give them autonomy, a sense of agency, and responsibilities. Another time, my younger son said, "I've been taking the garbage out for three years. Do you think I could do something else?" We reviewed the list of chores and started a rotation with each person shifting their duties from one week to the next. This was a way to make them feel heard, to give them a say, while still having them participate and contribute to the life of the household.

At one time we actually started doing a "Sunday circle," where we would talk about what did not work out for us during the week. We eventually stopped because it left Sunday night meals on a negative note. We said, "from now on if there is something that's on your mind, don't wait and save it for Sunday night; say it right away."

I do not think Alan and I were strict parents. Rather, we were quite accepting, and I believe that is why we maintained strong communication with our children. I never felt that we lost them, even throughout their teenage years. They always felt comfortable talking to us and telling us about their problems or when they had done something wrong. To this day, all three of them are fabulous communicators. Looking at it from the outside, I think they always felt loved, accepted, and encouraged, and understood that we believed in them and trusted them.

Alan and I still connect with each of our kids at least once a week, as well as with our grandchildren, especially the four eldest ones. If I leave a message today, I know I will hear back from them within twenty-four hours. They even ask for advice about how to deal with certain things. This connectedness gives me such joy. I adore them all. We have always been very involved in their lives. Naturally, we are closest to the two eldest ones, who live much closer to us. And I babysat the eldest for two years; that never leaves. But last summer, our two Vancouver grandsons spent five days with us and expressed the wish to repeat the experience this year. As for Alanis's kids, since they are so far away in California and still too young to fly over on their own, we communicate through FaceTime. Not unlike her parents, our daughter has chosen a non-traditional educational and parenting style for her children, one adapted to her unique situation. Alanis practises "unschooling" with her kids. It is a pedagogical discovery method that is driven by the child's interests. One of the reasons for this may be that while she did enjoy school, she also suffered because of her fame and felt excluded by her peers.

Over the years, we have also stayed in touch with our oldest son's ex-spouse, whom I call my daughter-in-love as opposed to my daughter-in-law. We were even invited to attend her second wedding. Alanis's husband and father of their kids is wonderful. He has truly been a rock for his family. He is very involved in his children's homeschooling while she is away on tour, or when they accompany her on tour as a family. I am so glad these significant others, both past and present, have been and are still part of my children's lives and of our lives as well. Thanks to them, we have all become better people and have wonderful grandchildren.

***

Music was part of our children's lives from a very early age. However, they did not inherit that interest or inclination from me. I believe talent skips generations. In my case, at least, that is what happened. While there was a piano at my house and in my grandparents' restaurant in Hungary, I never learned to play it. I did take three years of guitar lessons, but if you offered me a hundred dollars to play right now, I would say, "keep your money, it's not going to happen." It is safe to say that this experiment definitely did not work. Later in life, I was asked to teach music to Grade 5 and Grade 8 students. The supervisor from the head office knew I was struggling, so she came to teach a song to my Grade 5 students and told me that, when she would be back in a few days, she wanted to see me do the same lesson for the Grade 8 students. "That was interesting," she said, after hearing my lesson. Clearly, that was not a compliment. "Oh. How interesting was it?" I naively asked. "You sang the same song to four different tunes."

Alan was always much more interested in music than me. Growing up, music had always been a big part of his French-Canadian family culture, starting with his grandmother and his mother, who constantly listened to the radio. Ever since we met, I remember him listening to rock 'n' roll records and Top 40 radio hits. And as we travelled across Europe during our years in Germany, there was always music playing in the car or the camper as the soundtrack of our weekend adventures and summer discoveries. One weekend we went to Avignon in the south of France. Alan noticed that a cinema was showing the movie *Grease*, starring John Travolta and Olivia Newton-John, which he had heard about on a Canadian radio station playing on the military base. We decided to bring the kids. Back at the campground, I asked the children if they had enjoyed the movie. The response was quite enthusiastic. It was a hit! Then Alanis asked me, "Mom, do you have a microphone?" Of course, I was not in the habit of carrying a microphone around in the camper, so I told her that I did not have one. "But I'd like to sing some of those songs I heard in the movie." I did have a nail polish bottle with me. "Will this work if you pretend it's a microphone?" I asked, handing her the bottle. "Yes!" And she sang all the Olivia Newton-John songs. We could see the transformation in her, right before our eyes. It mirrored that of Sandy's character, which evolved from the demure high school girl to the confident young woman in leather. And it blew us away at the time. It was one of those key, unforgettable moments, which gave us a glimpse of what was to come. She wanted to sing and perform, and she had the talent for it. She was only three.

When we returned to Canada, it seemed only natural for our kids to participate in the school talent show. I particularly remember the three of them up on stage performing Queen's "Another One Bites the Dust." It was always a great pleasure to see them do something they enjoyed together, whether it was music, swimming, or even street hockey, knowing they would each go their own way soon. They also took up musical instruments. We had a piano at home and unexpectedly found a teacher one day at the music store. He was there as a customer talking to the clerk at the counter. When he mentioned that he had played the piano for nine years, we asked him if he would be willing to teach our children. That was enough for us, and we decided to hire him on the spot, even though he was not formally qualified as a piano instructor. He agreed to come directly to our house, which was much more convenient. As it turned out, he was also of Hungarian origin. Over time, he became part of the family and even had a key to the house. Everything was done informally. There was no schedule with him or with us. He would come early, late, whatever, it did not really matter. I still remember that for Alanis and Wade, who still could not read music, I had to somehow write down where the keys were and where to place their fingers. I was not into music myself, but I wanted to help. I also remember thinking that it could be very lonely for children to practise every day, so I would find a book and sit in the room where they played so they did not feel lonely. I was not paying complete attention, that is for sure, but at least they felt like they had an audience. After a year of lessons, Chad eventually decided that it was not really for him, and that was fine. The twins, on the other hand, definitely enjoyed piano.

One day, a few years later, Alanis called me from the kitchen where I was cooking. She said:

"Mom, come and hear a song I wrote."

I listened carefully.

"How did you come up with this, Alanis?" I asked, a little concerned about the rather mature content of the lyrics.

She explained that they were based on what she had heard on the radio. We had music playing all the time around the house, and we were surrounded by entertainment magazines, thanks to Alan. Our musician friends Jackie and Lindsay Morgan, whose concerts we regularly attended as Alanis watched and listened attentively at the entrance, were such a great influence. They mentored Alanis (and us) as she made her first steps in the music business, helping her produce a demo tape of that first song, "Found the Right Man at the Right Place," which came to the ears of local talent scout and recording artist manager John Alexander, who used to be the lead singer of the Ottawa rock band Octavian. He thought this nine-year-old girl showed promise but refused to sign her because she was too young. Still, he kept an eye out for her.

Around the same time, we travelled to Los Angeles as a family. Alan found one of those maps that showed tourists like us where all the major Hollywood stars lived. He asked Alanis:

"You like Olivia Newton-John, right? Here's a star map that shows where she lives. Would you like to go?"

"Oh, yeah, Dad, yeah, yeah."

"But don't think for one second that you're going to get to talk to her. You may get to speak to a security camera, but that's it."

Alan took her up there. He pointed to the camera and told her:

"Go ahead and talk to her; leave her a message."

She walked up, and said confidently:

"Hi Olivia. My name is Alanis and I'm going to be a big star, just like you."

This happened right in front of our eyes. That is when Alan told me:

"Okay, we have to do something about this. We are not going to spit into the wind."

***

We never tried to stop any of our children from pursuing something that they enjoyed or felt passionate about. Just like in our own professional lives, if an opportunity came along for one of them, we encouraged them to seize it; if a door opened to a new adventure, we walked through it together as a family. I was always part of the team. Never did Alan or I feel that supporting Alanis was too much for us or for our family. When she was ten, she met Dominic D'Arcy, Ottawa's "singing policeman," when he came to perform at her school. He was blown away by her voice and invited her and her twin brother Wade to accompany him and other child stars to performances around Ottawa and Ontario. That is when she started performing in hospitals, community centres, and shopping malls, and won all the singing contests she entered.

When she was eleven or twelve, Alanis, who was always hungry for more, asked her father, "Dad, what do I do now? What's next?" With his sharp business acumen, Alan responded: "Let's try TV or the theatre. You've got to learn some poise." She had never done any acting, though she had learned how to dance at Scarcella's dancing school. And so, she performed with the Orpheus Musical Theatre Society and played in *Annie*. We knew Ottawa newscaster Max Keeping very well. He informed us that they were doing auditions for the hit comedy television show *You Can't Do That on Television*, produced by the local CTV station but broadcast across North America on the major cable network Nickelodeon. The show featured kids being kids, performing sketches, and doing silly things like getting "slimed," which became the show's trademark. Max suggested that Alanis audition, and she made it. This was in 1986, and she stayed on for five episodes. I remember going to the first session with my twelve-year-old. I dropped her off and intended to go get groceries while she taped the show. I was not what we call today a "helicopter mom," that is for sure. But then I asked myself: "Do you really have to go get groceries right now? Shouldn't you rather be going in to support and cheer your daughter on?" Groceries never came home that day.

The song Alanis had written and performed in our front hall at age nine or ten eventually became her first single. Following the success of her television appearance, Alan brought her to Toronto to work with a producer; they recorded a couple of songs, which were released in 1987. This gave her some airtime in the city, which led to greater and better opportunities, like performing at Ottawa's Tulip Festival, where she met her first manager, Stephan Klovan. He quickly had her sing her own songs at fashion shows and perform the national anthem at local and national sporting events. Things were picking up but her career was still manageable. Were we stressed? We just figured, "Let's do it. If you want to do it, I want to see it." Alan was all in from day one. The extrovert in him enjoyed the spotlight and the media attention. He handled the press and cultivated contacts in the music industry. As more of an introvert, I was just along for the ride.

When our friend John Alexander over at MCA Publishing saw the demo video Alanis did that year, we asked him what he thought her next move should be. He responded: "Well, she's fifteen, and neither MCA nor any other label is going to take her on and record her because they don't want another Tiffany." MCA was looking for a songwriter, not just a singer or performer. They were interested in the rights to her songs. Since the publishing company was not prepared to invest in a one-hit wonder, they recommended we have her keep writing—that was the key. Alan suggested she go to Toronto and other places to do some co-writing with other songwriters. It was a big gamble. There were no guarantees of any sort, except belief. If you do not have belief, you do not do these things. Most importantly, Alanis had to believe. Which she did. She was talented and we, as parents, were unorthodox. Why would we ever stop somebody who was that passionate? We trusted John; he was smart and looked out for her best interest, but we were watching who else surrounded her. Success and recognition, especially at that young age, can attract toxic people. Alanis continued to work on her writing and to do auditions. At sixteen, she eventually appeared on the American television show *Star Search*, which gave her enough exposure to finally secure a record deal.

The two albums she released in 1991 and 1992 turned her into Canada's first teenage pop star. This was a lot for her. And for us as parents. Especially as educators, it confronts you when your children tell you they want to stop their formal schooling after high school. It is not how we originally saw things going. But we approached this in a very liberal way, I think. We encouraged our children to follow their dreams and gave them the freedom to achieve them because we trusted them and knew they were smart. If they were making all types of mistakes and bad decisions, we would have put our foot down, we would have intervened. But they never did. Allowing them to become adults is a journey on which we accompany them, a process during which we learn to separate from them and become guides instead of teachers.

Alanis moved to Toronto in 1992 when she was eighteen after her first two albums. That year, she proudly sang the national anthem for the inaugural game of the Ottawa Senators hockey team, just as she had the privilege of singing it again in the summer of 2026 at the World Cup opening-day ceremony in Toronto. Seeing how she had gone as far as she could in Canada, her manager Scott Welch told us:

"Georgia and Alan, if anything is going to happen with Alanis, you have to let her go."

"Where?" Alan asked.

"To Los Angeles."

That was a tough one, both for Alan and me. She was still eighteen.

"If you don't, it's over," Scott added.

It was overwhelming and heart-wrenching, but also incredibly exciting at the same time. We could not accompany her since we were working, but we trusted

Scott. That is the whole point of trust. In the long run, many kids who come into the entertainment industry do not make it because their parents will not let them go. They want to go with them and be there every single minute, every step of the way. But music companies do not want to hire the parents. Parents end up getting in the way of their children. We did not do that. We trusted the people around Alanis. The people we trusted set her up with people they trusted. It formed a chain of trust, which protected her all those years.

And so, she went to LA. She started making friends with key people. But Alan kept asking John Alexander the same question he had been asking him for years:

"When will she start making some money?"

For herself, not for everybody else. Alan wanted our children to learn about and enjoy financial independence. John tried to reassure us by telling us that MCA would be taking care of her in the United States. In March 1994, MCA Publishing introduced Alanis to Glen Ballard. Together, they wrote the *Jagged Little Pill* album, which was released the following year. I would be lying if I said the language and themes of her songs were not a bit of a surprise (not to say shock) to both Alan and me. Nothing good Catholic parents would approve of, that is for sure. But we were not about to object and say, "I'm sorry, dear, you're not putting that in." Alan and I learned a long time ago that whoever writes the song is the one who has the final say. We always believed that if it is your intention to send a specific message in a specific way, who are we to say "No, no, no, that's not acceptable." There was no stopping her anyway.

One night, after the album had become an international hit, John invited us to a restaurant in Santa Monica, on Ocean Boulevard. He got to the point.

"Alan," said John, "you've been bugging me for years. Leave me alone about the money!"

"Well," responded Alan, "until I see my daughter is taken care of properly, I'll keep pestering you."

John paused, reached into his jacket pocket, and pulled out an envelope.

"That's your first cheque."

A million dollars. Alan still teases me with this story because I had forgotten that small detail.

***

While Alanis was well surrounded throughout her early career, not everything was perfect. In fact, there were horror stories. She was robbed at gunpoint on the streets of Los Angeles. She had the sole copy of the *Jagged Little Pill* album in her purse. She and Glen had just finished writing the lyrics. Luckily, the thieves were only interested in her wallet and left the purse. Had they stolen the purse with all its contents, her story would have been quite different. Other things happened to

Alanis as well, in Ottawa as well as in LA, but those are not my stories to tell. With people we trusted. We still have resentment about these issues, but strive to let go of the anger. But it was not only Alanis. Our other children also experienced some difficult things. Some of them Alan and I might have been able to prevent, but one can never fully protect one's child. Still, we were devastated to have failed in our duty to protect. I—we—bitterly regret that we did not have the chance to fully protect our kids, and that will haunt me for the rest of my life. How does a parent continue to trust people, to trust one's child, without becoming overprotective? What did I learn from all this? Continue to trust, but be more cautious, of course. Do not do anything that does not feel comfortable to you. Make sure you go to bed at night feeling you were your best self in dealing with whatever it is that life throws at you.

Alanis also struggled with eating disorders throughout her teenage years, because she was trying to work in an industry that demanded young girls to be slim. There was so much pressure about looks and being onstage. What consoles me—if consolation is to be had—is the fact that at least some good came out of something bad: She had a place to channel and share her pain—her music. In a way, it is comforting to know that Alanis had the strength to make something beautiful that also helps others.

Alanis's meteoric rise brought her international fame and superstardom status. What a ride that was, in those early days. After all Alanis's hard work, the world finally took notice and, suddenly, she had sold over a million albums. Alan enjoyed the showbiz aspects. The boys and I, much less so. I remember going to the bank one day and asking the teller if I could change the name on my credit card to avoid attracting unwanted attention as I was going about my daily business. Alanis's career really impacted her brothers. It was hard on them. People would see Wade and say:

"That's Alanis Morissette's brother over there!"

They did the same thing to Chad.

"You must be so happy to be her brother!"

Their sister's international fame definitely shone a light on us all, but on the boys in particular. So while the boys were, of course, happy to be Alanis's brothers, they were not happy about this unwanted attention. That part was not pleasant. How could Alan and I protect the boys? Well, we could not, really. But we could help them become more resilient and impervious to the limelight. We told them not to give their power away. We encouraged them to find their own path. That was, of course, easier said than done, but they had the personality and strength to go and discover their own mission. I am so proud of them and how they have shown up in the world, on their own terms, on their own paths.

***

All three of our children left the house at eighteen, each one to pursue a passion or a dream. And we let them go. That was part of the trust we had in them and the relationship we had built with them. As I think back on this, I believe that one of the things that worked for us to cultivate connection with our children was to accept them and follow them as they each pursued their own interests. I would ask them: "Is that what speaks to you, what inspires you to be the best self you can be?" I cannot count the number of times I have repeated that to them. Chad went off to work in business, first in Montreal, then in Toronto. A few years later, the twins decided to leave home to each start their own lives, one in Toronto then in LA, and the other in India. With "vagabondish" parents like us who dragged them across Europe and North America since they were toddlers, I cannot really say that it was a big surprise for us to see them travel and live in different parts of the world. It was part of our lifestyle, which we passed on to our children. Before they left, we had a chat with each one of them. What will you do? How will you do it? We were, of course, somewhat apprehensive, but that was part of the process of letting go and making them responsible and accountable for their own lives. Alan sometimes jokes that the kids were really quite lucky to have us as parents. He jests, of course, but it is true in many ways. They were allowed and trusted to try things. But they also had to hold their end of that bargain: They had to prove themselves to us—with their intelligence and with the choices they made. Ultimately, I think we transferred our open and unusual (for the time) style of teaching to our style of parenting. Just like we have never been afraid to start over in our professional lives. Some call it crazy; I call it courage. That is just the way we are. Our three kids saw that growing up. Change does not scare them; they know something good will come of it. But they each had to find and forge their own path.

Our eldest son Chad created a North American brokerage business selling accomplished companies. Wade established himself as a yoga instructor with classes and studios in Vancouver, podcasts, and sales and marketing for Lululemon. Alanis succeeded in the entertainment industry as a world-renowned singer-songwriter. She has also become an activist and an advocate on questions of mental health, eating disorders, self-confidence, and female empowerment, participating in international conferences and organizing seminars or spiritual retreats around the world that focus on mindfulness, healing, and music. She even received an honorary doctorate from the University of Ottawa in 2025. Although such career choices might seem odd coming from children whose parents went to college and university to become teachers, we have always tried to teach our children to follow their talents with passion and hard work until they became successful at it. Education is found in life even more than in school experience.

For instance, Wade, in his teenage years, developed a strong and profound interest in yoga, a discipline that was not nearly as popular and common at the turn of the 1990s as it is today. Instead of looking for an instructor in Ottawa, Toronto, or maybe the United States, he decided to go over directly to India to study and train with Pattabhi Jois, a famous yoga guru. Not many eighteen-year-olds would think of going to India alone for three months, staying in ashrams, learning how to meditate for twenty-four hours, or going on a ten-day silent meditation retreat. One night while he was there, he called me around midnight. "Hi Mom. I'm at this number. I just wanted to check in. I'm safe, and..." Click. The line had been cut. Remembering this still gives me the shivers. I tried to call that number for two hours straight, but I could not get through. Finally, a woman answered.

"I need a miracle. My son called me two hours ago, but the line was cut. Do you remember him?"

"Oh yes, he's in the restaurant across the street. I can get the phone to him if you like."

I love the word *persevere*, and I think every one of our children has followed and lived by that word throughout their adult life.

I remember my mother's parting thoughts when she passed away: "I've done my best. It's time to rest." This was engraved onto her tombstone; Alan and I always remembered that. We cannot beat ourselves up about things that are now water under the proverbial bridge. There is no point.

And we are so proud of how the kids have each come into their own, despite, but also in many ways thanks to our unique parenting style.

9

Career Adventures: An Entrepreneur in Yoga Pants (1980–2000)

AFTER THREE YEARS in Germany, we returned to Canada on August 18, 1980, our suitcases filled with the memories of our many adventures, which would forever be embedded in our minds. This new chapter in our lives started with readjusting back to life in Canada, seeing our families once again, and moving to a new house in the Hunt Club area.

While we were away, my mother and sister graciously oversaw the preparation and decoration of our beautiful new home, ensuring it was ready for us to move into, as soon as we arrived.

Upon our return, Alan accepted a principalship, an opportunity that opened a new stage in his career in education. Before coming back, I had written to my school board asking if they would extend my leave of absence from teaching. This way I could stay home to care for my children, who were now nine and six. Unfortunately, my request was denied.

That is when I decided it was time for me to resign from my teaching career. For the first month or so, I looked forward to Chad, Alanis, and Wade coming home for lunch. We often shared interesting and lovely conversations. The kids had always been very comfortable communicating their feelings with me, and with each other.

One day, they shared their wish to have lunch at school instead of at home, as they were missing out on important play time with their friends during the break. There was no reason not to agree, and it was good for their autonomy. What would I do now with no teaching position and the kids at school all day?

I was not about to sit back and wait for things to happen. I still loved teaching, so I put my name on the supply teacher list. As it turned out, I realized that supply teaching was not exactly what I was looking for. Supply teachers are often challenged by the classes they cover. Most of it I could handle, but there were days when it was more than what I had bargained for. Once, in a special education class where the children were misbehaving, I remember putting my daybook down and telling them:

"Either you start getting along, or I'll have to leave. I can't take all this negativity."

9.1. In front of the house, August 1980.
Source: Family Collection.

The room went quiet. Then one of the kids said to me:

"Good for your, Miss. You expressed your feelings!"

In another special education class, a young boy once began to run around the classroom, dangerously wielding a protractor. I asked him seven times to stop and sit down. Then, because I was really concerned about his and his classmates' safety, I grabbed his shoulders and pushed him down to sit at his desk. He yelled:

"Don't you treat me like a dog!"

I told him I would happily treat him as a young boy if he were not endangering himself and others.

As I left after that day, I asked myself: "Do you still want to keep teaching this way?" I remember thinking, "I would rather eat glass and die than keep doing this."

* * *

I tried being a Welcome Wagon representative, where you advertise local businesses to new neighbours by giving them gift certificates to encourage them to use those businesses. My new boss explained that we would need ten gift certificates from ten companies for me to begin my visits. She wanted to see if I could secure these.

I did.

The next morning, she asked if I had managed to find any businesses interested. I gave her the first one and when we went in, the sale was closed in minutes. The same held true for the second and third businesses. She marvelled at how easily each business had agreed, saying she had never experienced anything like this before. I told her that it was an easy decision for them, since I already set everything up the day before.

"How many did you set up?" she asked, very surprised.

"Ten, like you asked."

She then shared with me that she was meant to come and show me how to court and convince these businesses. Never in all her years was it already a done deal, except for the paperwork.

I could do this type of work, and do it well, but I felt incomplete. It was not stimulating enough and did not speak to my heart. It was time to find something that would keep my interest and excitement alive. Still, this experience made me realize I was good at talking and interacting with people. Gradually, I transitioned from my refugee reticence to the exuberant and confident self that I had been until I left Hungary. The real Georgia was back! I felt alive and ready to take on any challenge.

That is when I decided to become a fitness instructor. Since I was already a trained physical education teacher, switching to this promised to be relatively easy. Sports and physical activity had been appealing to me since growing up in Budapest. It was not full-time at this stage, so I was still able to experience being a housewife and a mother. I could be home to greet everyone with joy after their long days at school and work. However, teaching only a few fitness classes a week was not filling my schedule or fulfilling my hyperactive nature.

Then came an unexpected connection with a Mary Kay Cosmetics sales director. I was already using some of the Mary Kay products, such as facial cleansers, moisturizers, and others. She was a very good salesperson because she convinced me to become a representative. Although I found myself to be a very slow learner in the beginning, this gave me a chance to learn sales.

To start out, I bought $3,000 worth of products, and since I did not want to impose on my circle of friends, I created homemade business cards. This way, clients could call me and book an appointment for a free facial. I would simply hand out the cards to strangers and walk away before they could say anything. Needless to say, I did not sell much that way. What I did do, however, was give a lot of cosmetics as Christmas gifts or birthday presents. The following July, almost a year after I had been in business, I invited my best girlfriends over to try a facial and come for lunch. After the facial, I never closed the sale. I simply thanked them:

"It's wonderful that you took the time to see the business I started."

My friends immediately stopped me.

"This is wonderful! How can we buy these products? How long have you been doing this? How did you become so good in such a short period of time?"

"Oh, I began a year ago, not just now."

They then asked me why it took me a whole year to invite them over. It was statements like these from my friends that reminded me to come out of my shell and get out of my own way in order to be successful in this career.

As of that following September, I decided to attend Monday meetings and learn how to do things correctly with proven sales techniques. Interestingly, during one of those training sessions, the speaker asked the audience:

"If you haven't reached your goal with our business, please stand up."

I stood up, ashamed.

"What is your goal?"

I had decided privately that I would like to win the car offered by the company to those who reached a predetermined sales target.

"By when?"

It was September and my birthday was in July. I thought this gave me enough time.

"By my birthday, in July."

It is amazing what happens when you set goals and work a system with enthusiasm. I had the car by Christmas! That was the best training; it unlocked my potential and unleashed my sales and marketing acumen. I carried on with this career for four years, building a small sales team. Yet something was still missing. Somehow, my career in cosmetics did not speak to my soul and I began to lose interest, even though I continued to believe in the products and still use many of them to this day.

One day in 1989, as I was taking a walk in our neighbourhood, someone from the next street over asked me if I was the Hungarian living in the area.

"I've been wanting to meet with you because I also have a Hungarian background."

This opened the door to a new friendship. Over the course of our conversations, she shared her story. She was working for an American company out of Memphis, Tennessee, where she marketed and sold environmental products, such as air and water filtration systems, while building her own sales force. She needed help with sales and marketing, and my interest had been piqued, so I signed on to her team. My experience in cosmetics had solidified my confidence in selling and training.

This business not only captured my interest and corresponded to my values, but Alan's as well. I explored the role full-time, and Alan joined in on a part-time basis. We worked together as a team.

There were two aspects to our business, selling products and building a team to help with sales. The results of this entrepreneurial adventure went beyond our expectations. At some point, Alan had to choose between staying on part-time or switching to full-time. He was drawing in more money part-time than he was making in his full-time position as a principal. And he was having much more fun. The choice was obvious, and easy. He resigned from the principalship and came on board full-time.

For the next two years (1990–1991), we reached the highest pay levels in the company as national marketing directors. Our business grew both in Canada and in the United States. We introduced the business to our eighteen-year-old son Chad, who used it to cut his teeth, so to speak, in the world of entrepreneurial economics. This was the beginning of our son's foray into business and entrepreneurship, which he has embraced very successfully to the present day. Over the years, he has developed a career as a business broker buying and selling businesses in Canada and the United States that generate revenues of at least a million dollars. However, the severe recession of the early 1990s affected the sale of products and therefore the entire industry. Alan always had a backup plan. Since he had been a French teacher in the past, he knew he could return to education, which he did from the latter part of 1992 until his retirement in 2016.

As for me, my new, uninhibited self definitely enjoyed the world of business and the personal freedom that it could offer. As a result, I took on another sales career with a utility auditing company that sold energy and telecommunications expense auditing packages to major corporations in North America. My main role in the business was to speak to controllers and CEOs of major corporations to help them cut utility and telecommunication expenses to increase their bottom line. The challenge was to get a meeting with these executives. By then, I knew how to break through the "gatekeepers" who would or would not put me through to the correct person.

My presentation to these CEOs was a nine-page script, which I could not and did not feel I needed to memorize. The corporate heads were very busy individuals, so I put yellow sticky notes on my presentation folder pages. A supervisor came from Montreal to check and see how I was conducting my presentations. When he saw my yellow sticky notes during one of my appointments, he was totally appalled. I remember being scolded and told that it was disrespectful to present in this manner. He said not to approach any other big companies until I had the entire script memorized. I objected:

"But Bell Northern Research [BNR] wants to see me for a second appointment."

He was completely flabbergasted!

"You mean you took this 'shitty' presentation of yours to him and he wants to see you again?"

"That's right!"

To the supervisor's total surprise, on that second appointment I signed the biggest contract since 1933. Not only did BNR sign for Canada but they also signed for the United States. I was given a $1,000 bonus for making the biggest sale ever in the company's history. I continued to do things my way and did quite well for the next two years. I always believed that you had to be direct and cut to the chase when dealing with busy people. It certainly paid off in this case.

One day at the end of the 1990s, I remember reading an article that talked about how children laugh four hundred times a day while adults do it only fifteen times. That particular day, I had only laughed twice. When I got home, I discussed with Alan how I felt. We have always been supportive of each other, both in our daily lives as well as in our business decisions. I needed to move on to a job where I could really be myself, not have to dress up in a suit with a briefcase, and not have to beg for appointments with CEOs. So I called up my boss, the head of the company, and told him I was resigning. Out of courtesy, I offered to stay for two weeks if they wanted me to. He did not understand.

"Why would you quit when you are number thirty-nine out of four hundred representatives? You have been working very well in the company, and if you stopped visiting your twins on the West Coast, you would be my number one."

"I am good at this position, I know, but I'm not enjoying it. I can't laugh and I love to laugh."

"Nobody has ever resigned from a job for that reason."

Well, apparently, now someone had.

⋆ ⋆ ⋆

Alan describes this part of my life as a "floundering period." I was looking for another way to contribute meaningfully, one that I believed in, that I loved, and that I was good at. It was the year 2000 and it was time for me to ground myself into a fulfilling career that really allowed me to help others. It was also at this time that, at the recommendation of my family doctor—who had predicted I would be in a wheelchair by age sixty-five if I did nothing—I started taking yoga classes for back issues I had been struggling with since my youth. A few months later, I received a call from a friend of my son Chad, who owned a local fitness club and had a yoga show on CTV Ottawa. Looking to broaden both his customer base and his audience, he asked me to teach a seven-minute chair yoga session on his show. I am usually a daring person who jumps at any new opportunity that comes along, but I put this invitation off for three months.

I did not think I was ready to do classes on television, since I was not a fully qualified yoga instructor yet. But this was not the first challenge I faced in my life journey. I finally mustered the courage and the confidence to do the segment. Despite a few mishaps with the lapel microphone, which I did not properly use, it seems I did a good enough job for the fitness club owner to invite me to join his studio and teach yoga.

This decision became a new defining moment and a new turning point in my life.

Only two people showed up for my first class: my sister (with a bouquet of flowers) and another person. I instructed the entire class sitting down, hoping it would not show that I was not an experienced yoga teacher and that I did not really know what I was doing.

That is when I asked our son Wade in Vancouver, who was already offering a variety of yoga training programs all over the world, to take me under his wing and teach me how to understand and teach yoga. Seeing how I was first a physical education teacher, then a fitness instructor, I figured transitioning into a Hatha yoga teacher would come easily. I just needed to learn the correct postures and sequences. That training and experience definitely ignited a passion for yoga, which opened a new door and a new career for me. I will always be grateful to my younger son for agreeing to come to Ottawa to train me (and eight of my friends), and for persuading me to further explore and pursue this lovely practice.

My first goal was to set up a studio in the basement of our home. I literally went from door to door, inviting my neighbours to come and take yoga classes with me. Even though by the fourth house I felt like a salesperson begging people to buy their product, I persevered and carried on until I had ten people committed to coming. Monday night classes started a week later and lasted for over twenty years, until COVID hit in 2020. We had many great sessions in that downstairs yoga studio, where I also held several day-long retreats (usually from 9 a.m. to 3 p.m.). We would begin with a yoga class then we would discuss self-esteem. After lunch, we would do a dance to invigorate ourselves and then move on to different meditation techniques. The feedback was always extremely positive. What came out of those retreat days was that we wanted our connection to be more than just about yoga. So we started to meet every month as a group of friends and share on different topics.

We even went away on longer retreats together, learning about each other and enjoying such wonderful female bonding experiences.

Business as a yoga instructor started to boom yet it still remained a part-time occupation. It was the year 2000 and I was busy babysitting my newborn grandson two days a week, while working from home the other three as his father Chad's marketing assistant. As my life and interest for the discipline continued to grow, Wade began to show me how the business of yoga was run.

I felt it was time for me to really embrace my love for yoga and expand from teaching only Hatha in my home and at various fitness centres around Ottawa. Since one of my favourite areas was pain management, I decided to create a chair yoga program for seniors. My oldest student was 106 years old and did all the exercises in a wheelchair. By 2003, I was not only offering chair yoga classes in thirty-two seniors' residences and long-term care units, but I had developed a manual and training program to form a team who could spread wellness in several senior homes. This activity was well received among Alzheimer's patients as well. My mission with this large-scale outreach effort was and continues to be to provide yoga for all ages, and to promote physical health and well-being while building the confidence and self-esteem of the elderly in our community.

Whatever positive impact this activity may have had on the seniors who took my classes, whether physical or psychological, those very special students also left their mark on me. I particularly remember one new member in my chair yoga class, who claimed to have just moved into the nursing home the same morning. Although she was wearing a wig and was in a wheelchair, she did everything that I initiated in the class and was smiling most of the time. I began to doubt if I had heard her right that she had just moved in. Usually, it takes three months or more for a senior to feel they belong in a residence, rather than the home they left behind, and begin to mingle with other residents or take part in activities. At the end of the session, I walked over to speak to her privately and asked if she had indeed arrived that very morning. She confirmed.

"How can you be so positive on your first day of your transition from home?" I wondered.

She answered with three simple words.

"Acknowledge. Accept. Adjust."

Over the years, those three simple yet impactful words have helped me deal and cope with change on numerous occasions. That conversation was so empowering for me that I had the three words written on rocks and have handed them out over four hundred times. As with everything else, my impulse is to give back and share with others the teachings or insights life has offered me.

Since I was a certified teacher, I was hired by many school boards to teach children's classes in various schools. I also gave yoga classes to teachers after school hours. It was calming for them and fun for me to find myself in a school environment once again, without having to worry about giving detentions, marking papers, or doing report cards. One thing I observed in the children's classes was that many times when we came to *Shavasana* (the only term I know in Sanskrit), which is the lie down meditation part at the end of the session, about twenty-five percent of the class would fidget and constantly move around. When I realized this, I asked any child who was having difficulty remaining still at the end of the yoga class to put their hands up. My hand went up as well. Then I asked

Yoga for All

A Profile of Georgia Morissette

by Kate Reid

Sitting in a circle, nine women look expectantly toward the door. They live in a seniors' residence and range in age from seventy-five to over ninety. Most are in chairs but their walkers are close at hand; one stays in her wheelchair. They are waiting for their yoga teacher.

16 • COMPLETE HEALTH • *Summer 2003*

9.2. *Complete Health* magazine, summer, 2003.
Source: Complete Health.

them to follow the next word I was going to say, which was "freeze"! They all stopped immediately, as if they were statues. That is when I told them:

"You are the boss of you. You can say 'freeze' at any moment, whether it's to stop yourself from yelling, talking, screaming, laughing, or moving. You are the boss of you!"

Over the next week, several students from that school came up to me and said:

"Thank you for that freeze lesson. I usually had a hard time falling asleep at night because I was tossing and turning and moving about in my bed, but now I just say 'freeze.' Then I stop myself and fall asleep easily."

I felt empowered as a teacher again. I was once more able to make a difference in the lives of these kids.

One day a gentleman I knew, whose family members had participated in my yoga sessions, asked me a challenging question.

"Would you teach my basketball team of twelve seventeen-year-old boys a ten-week course?"

I was not thrilled, initially.

"Would your team appreciate a grandmother teaching them yoga for ten weeks?"

"You have taught my daughters in the children's classes you ran, and then you also had my mother and my wife in your Monday classes, and from what I hear you would be ideal for my team."

That opened my mind and convinced me to accept, even though I was somewhat doubtful that it would work, and that a dozen tall teenage boys, their two coaches, and the coaches' younger son, would all fit in my basement yoga room for ten.

Throughout all these experiences and encounters with people young and old, my authentic self was finally shining through and beginning to be nurtured. I had found my essence in the versatility and freedom of working for myself by doing business in the healing arts.

Personally, as well as professionally, this path has been so fulfilling that I have continued to passionately follow yoga as a career to this day.

10

Travelling My Way Back to Me: A Journey of Self-Discovery (2000–2024)

BEFORE THE ARRIVAL of the new millennium, there was one faraway adventure that is worth mentioning because of the tremendous and defining impact it had on my life journey.

It began in 1997, when my daughter Alanis planned a trip to help the orphans of India. After two years of touring around the world and a gruelling schedule, she was mentally and physically exhausted and wanted to reconnect in a place that she and her twin brother always perceived as very spiritual. The idea was that three adult women from our family—my sister Kati, my sister-in-law Carol, and myself—along with three young women of the next generation—Alanis and her two friends, Heather and Joanna—were to go help out in the orphanages of Kolkata (Calcutta) run by Mother Teresa.

We called it the "Goddesses Tour."

A great deal of preparation preceded our trip. We had to get our visas, update our immunization records, and gather all kinds of gifts to hand out to the children. When we finally completed all the necessary procedures and had our plane tickets arranged, we were informed that Mother Teresa had died.

This could hardly be. She seemed immortal, beyond time.

This terrible news only strengthened our resolve to help during these difficult times. We left in the early days of 1998. The flight from Ottawa to New Delhi and then to Kolkata was an exhausting experience. But before we could head to the lovely Kolkata hotel awaiting us, we were forced to stay cooped up on the plane for an additional seven hours.

That was nothing compared to what we saw afterwards, which left a profound mark on us all.

On our way to the first orphanage, we saw so many people sitting on the ground, hands out. Beggars asking for money repeatedly patted us on the shoulder. Cows walked haphazardly in the streets. We were overwhelmed. We could not wrap our heads around this brand-new world.

The second shock came soon thereafter.

In the first orphanage, I was shown into a room with a crib that slept not one, but six toddlers, with arms and legs hanging over the sides. In the next room, each one of us was handed a toddler to hold. I immediately noticed that the backs of the children's heads were flat. When I asked why, I was told that it was because they were mostly left lying in their cribs or beds for long periods of time.

"We don't have enough people to hold them and be with them," one staff member explained. "It's easy to criticize what is happening. You come here for a week or two and then you go back to your cushy lives. We live and work in these conditions daily."

Her forthright response has stayed with me to this very day as a stinging reminder of our blindness to the reality and suffering of other parts of the world.

At the next orphanage, we were each given a youngster to hold and were asked to take them to another room, where they were showing a Christmas video. The video cut out or went blank many times. As I watched the video with a little boy in my arms, I was surrounded by five more children who snuggled up to me. When I looked at the child on my side, I noticed something familiar on her wrist. It was the artificial hair piece I was wearing to enhance my style. That put things in perspective for me and taught me to let go of both my ego and my vanity.

Another location we visited housed school-aged girls and boys. Most of them had shaved heads for lice prevention. When they lined up to receive our gifts, I noticed that they were perfectly behaved. I asked if there was a specific reason for that. The nuns in charge pointed to a cage, which was occupied by two big black dogs. Apparently, if a child caused trouble, they were put in the cage. I was stunned and speechless.

But what floored me emotionally was seeing the nuns, as part of their regular morning routine, check the large garbage dumpsters to gather any abandoned babies that might still be alive. Would these children ever adjust to the trauma inflicted upon them?

During the final leg of our trip, four young boys became our guides. We took them out to eat and they showed us new sites. One of these was a spot by the Ganges River where we could view burial ceremonies from a distance. We watched silently as a group solemnly burned the body of a deceased loved one, then set the ashes afloat, surrounded by candles. That deeply spiritual event is still vivid in my memory.

When our young guides understood we were leaving the next day, they told us they were hoping we would sponsor them and keep sending money to them from abroad to support their education. They said that without our input they would be forced to sell walnuts on street corners to feed themselves and make a living. This broke my heart, but we were not in a position to do this.

When I came back to Canada after two extremely intense and draining weeks, my brain shut down. I reverted to the introvert, quiet person I had been after we escaped from Hungary. It took me four months to emerge emotionally from this experience and return to the real me. This trip influenced my life to a point I could not imagine, bringing out a level of empathy and compassion I did not suspect I had in me. Over the next twenty plus years, I found my calling by incorporating my adventures and their lessons into what I would call "my true authenticity." I wanted to help people no matter who they were and which life challenges they faced.

* * *

By the year 2000, Alan had found himself in several teaching positions across the city of Ottawa, and I was constantly evaluating and re-evaluating what I wanted to do next in my search for a fulfilling career. Over the course of the new millennium, I fulfilled, to a greater extent, these life choices of yoga, fitness instruction, travel adventures, life coaching, and overall physical, mental, and spiritual wellness.

This also included an all-encompassing enthusiasm for supporting my growing family. By 2019, we had the great fortune to have seven grandchildren. Over the years, we have crossed the country and the continent on several occasions to attend births or celebrate birthdays. This has allowed us to develop a bond and a connection with each of these wonderful grandchildren. Nowadays, thanks to technology, we regularly communicate with them on social media and, now that they are older, they drop in when their travels or those of their parents include coming to Ottawa. As I embraced my role as a grandparent, I lost sight and let go of my exuberant self at some point, buying into what I perceived was the socially accepted role and image of a grandmother. This included dressing more conservatively and wearing dull colours. When I realized that this self-imposed norm kept me from being myself, I went back to my colourful and sometimes whimsical wardrobe. It is not because you are a grandmother that you need to look like one!

* * *

After returning from Germany, I became known for helping others. In whatever role I found myself, my life choices were based on passion, discovery, and learning, and fuelled by a desire to effect positive action. In other words, my goals and desires were to give to others rather than to receive.

During a gift exchange, I was struck by the absurdity and waste of this gift-giving practice everyone mindlessly followed—including myself—simply because of social conventions. The intention behind the practice had been lost, though each person yearned to show their love and appreciation.

I asked each one of those forty people whether they would agree to abandon the gift exchange tradition, except for children. I added that if they really did wish to offer me something, they might consider making a donation to a charitable cause. I was immensely grateful that they accepted this proposal.

With this new tradition in place, we were able to sponsor several women who had experienced intimate partner violence and their children to provide them with a nice Christmas. We did this for seven years. I began receiving checks from complete strangers, which allowed us to provide twenty-one families with substantial gift certificates from local grocery and retail stores.

My favourite part of this project was when we delivered the certificates and extra gifts to the families. I also went to some of the women's shelters to teach them chair yoga and share some positivity.

One year, two young mothers had said they would each love a winter coat and a warm sweater. Since I was running short on time the morning I was to visit them, I took a suitcase and filled it with some sweaters and a few winter jackets of my own. When I met up with the two young mothers, I opened the suitcase for them to take whatever they fancied. They pulled out items and, one by one, rejected my collection, arguing that it was either too old-fashioned, not their favourite colour, or something else. I naively thought that my own personal tastes would suit theirs, and quickly understood that I had been sorely mistaken. I was immediately brought back to the image of my father shining shoes. Charity is never easy to accept, and people are proud no matter the circumstances. I invited them each to pick a coat and a sweater of their choice at a second-hand store. They were delighted and found exactly what they needed and wanted. Still, I was acutely reminded about the importance of supporting people while respecting their personal choices.

This desire to help others extended beyond charitable work. Word started to spread around to yoga communities in the Ottawa area, reaching as far as Elliot Lake, Ontario, where I was asked to do a chair yoga training for the staff of a seniors' home. Community centres in other cities also invited me to train their staff to teach Hatha yoga, mom and baby yoga, or parent and toddler yoga for after-school programs. Soon thereafter, there were too many classes for me to teach, so I ended up training other people to teach chair yoga. I would train them for free and when they showed me they could do this on their own, I would certify them. They then had the choice to find their own jobs and careers in the field or supply teach for me when I could not cover classes. After one of my classes in Russell, Ontario, I walked into a store where a vivacious woman was speaking with other customers. I remember thinking that she would make an amazing chair yoga teacher for seniors. I pressed my courage button, walked up to her, and asked her if she would consider it.

"Tell me more. That sounds awesome!" she responded enthusiastically.

Little did I know that she was a single mother working more than one job to keep providing for her six-year-old daughter. After our conversation, she did the training and took over two of my commitments. She was able to bring her daughter along, since classes were in the early evenings. She carried on with this for two years and is now the proud owner of a fitness studio, teaching yoga and fitness classes in resorts all over North America.

It warms my heart to know my reaching out to this woman that day in the store ended up having such a big impact on her life.

My journey within had prepared me for my journey without.

I describe this return to my inner self as a heroic passage from personal self-actualization and transcendent community actions to quite simply helping everyone and anyone. I believe that we need to make a difference in someone's life each day. A video that I used with my students when I was teaching showed an older man going into town to get his groceries every Saturday. He would take ten one-dollar bills (they still existed at the time), walk down the main street, and randomly drop each one of those bills along the way. When asked what he was he doing and why, he responded:

"I am proving that I am still here and that I can make a difference to ten people every Saturday."

It is interesting to see who or what can impact one's life if we remain open to it. In the same way, one never knows what difference one can make in someone else's life.

Another video I showed my students still lingers in my heart and memory. In it an older man sits on a park bench. A boy taps him on the shoulder.

"Sir," he asks, "could you tell me what time it is?"

The man responds. After the boy leaves, the man comments:

"That's the first time I had human touch in seven years."

That story has inspired me to always make a point of reaching out to at least one person a day with a smile, a wave, or an encouraging email.

* * *

As my yoga business expanded, I was and still am privileged to have found a great team to work with, which has given me the freedom to travel to see family and live new adventures.

Alan and I enjoyed many vacations in the first decade of the 2000s. Indeed, with the growth of our family, we now had more people to see and more places to go. The biggest novelty was having four grandsons from the marriages of our two sons. To this day we share a great connection with each one of them, even though they now all live in different cities and different countries.

Our eldest son was working in Naples, Florida, and I recall that one year he and his wife asked us not once, but four times, to join them for Christmas. We felt wanted. As our younger son started his family, we were yet again invited several times to join his family in Vancouver. At first, I would often go out West by myself, since Alan was still teaching. When he retired, we went back and forth to see both our sons and their families. I remember thinking at one point that Vancouver would be a great place to live, until we realized that it rained a lot there, and I knew Alan wanted more rather than less sunlight as he grew older.

Then came the great news that our daughter Alanis, who lived in California, was ready to give birth to her first child. We were happy to welcome a boy once again. After five grandsons, we were overjoyed when a granddaughter finally came along, thanks to Alanis once again. And to top it all off, she gave us one more boy to round out our half-dozen. They are all such amazing gifts! Our cup overflows.

The strong bond with our three children and now seven grandchildren carried on into the second decade of the 2000s. How we wished they all lived closer to us. Yet we count our blessings and feel so grateful that video calls and text messages can connect us anytime, anywhere.

* * *

I was always told that travel is life and education, all rolled into one. In my case, it has also pushed me out of my comfort zone to overcome my fears and be open to whatever comes next, whether new experiences or new friends.

Alan has always been the driving force behind our trips, always suggesting new adventures. Way back when we had our children at home, he would have our March break adventure planned out by Christmas time. And while we were on that trip, he would outline the plans for our summer holiday. I greatly appreciated my husband's sense of initiative, since I was not the best at researching destination opportunities. I was happy to just pack the necessary luggage and enjoy the ride.

One such memorable trip was to Sedona, Arizona. We went on a guided tour and hit it off with a lady with whom we shared some common interests. That evening we realized that she and her husband were both staying at the same hotel as we were. We became friends and have kept in touch over the years. They came to see us and stayed with us in Ottawa, inviting us in return to their home in Manchester, United Kingdom. Moreover, when we visited our dear friends in England—the one who had been a student of mine in Germany—the couple from Sedona came over and joined us for a weekend. The two have become friends ever since. This fortuitous development and new relationship could only have come about through travel and our connection with each couple on a number of levels.

Another friendship, this one with a young woman I met in one of my yoga classes, eventually brought us to Dallas, Texas, where we were invited to meet her children. From there, we went to San Antonio to celebrate our thirty-seventh wedding anniversary, where we strolled along the Riverwalk and into the fabulous

10.1. and 10.2. Yoga in Fiji with Alanis and Wade, 2001.
Source: Family Collection.

restaurants, which offered a great respite from the unbearable heat. At one point, we entered an office building to cool down. When asked if we had an appointment, I facetiously replied:

"Yes please, with your air conditioner!"

We had never been thrown out of a building before. Now I know better.

Alan's sensation seeking and his curiosity for the exotic, which have always been predominant traits of his personality, brought us once to the Pacific island of Fiji. Not only were we fortunate enough to have our twins travel with us, but I was unexpectedly asked by our host to share my yoga teaching with a dozen youngsters during our stay.

We were also invited on a river float expedition, which entailed wearing a wet suit, a life jacket, and flippers. This all sounded very exciting, but it was not for me, since I have always been afraid of water after almost drowning in Grade 7. I was truly ready to decline when I shared my fear with our twins, both great swimmers, who encouraged me in unison and assured me they would watch over me. It was an unforgettable adventure. We floated up the tributary river with an affluent high tide, watching huts and locals on the shore. We reached a lake and then proceeded to have the low tide bring us back to our starting point. That unique experience will always stay in my heart as an exceptional memory of how I conquered my personal fear of water and of not being in control thanks to the love and care of my family.

Another time, my dear friend Joan, who had serious health issues and was in a wheelchair at the time, her husband Mervin pushing and guiding her to their destination, taught me a lesson about the importance of really seeing and acknowledging people. Whenever we would meet with them, she mentioned how she had noticed that we were among their rare friends who genuinely cared and asked her how she was doing, instead of just inquiring about her husband and acting as if she was not there. For her, this meant a lot. As she recovered, they asked us to go on a canoe and portage trip with them across Algonquin Provincial Park, with its thousands of lakes, countless maple hills, and infinite rocky ridges. We portaged, canoed, and camped for several days. This was totally new (and quite demanding) for us, but we never turned down a challenge and were more than happy to follow along. Overall, it was an amazing experience, even if it was not necessarily my "natural environment."

In 2013, our eldest son invited us to Italy, where his fiancée was participating in a soccer tournament. At that time, our two eldest grandsons were thirteen and ten. It was one of our best times in Europe together. We stayed in a town called Stresa. The hotel owners were two brothers who gave us the most amazing welcome. When we arrived, they suggested we unpack and then return for a light supper on the house. How unexpected! Then, one weekend, we decided to go on an excursion to Mont Blanc, on the border between France and Italy, for which none

10.3. Algonquin Park, early 2000s.
Source: Family Collection.

of us were adequately prepared. When we asked our dear owners what we could do about it, they mentioned that there was plenty of warm clothing for us to use in the lobby. That literally made our day. After some more travelling, we decided to return to our favourite hotel for our last night in Italy. When we got there, they had a table set up just for us with a full meal and a bottle of wine waiting. These were some of the random acts of kindness and generosity towards others we experienced on that trip that made our stay unforgettable, and that have inspired me ever since.

A grandmother I met years ago shared that, when her grandchildren turned thirteen, she would treat them to a week-long holiday in the location of their choice. Alan and I liked the idea, and while we regret not having been able to bring any of them to Hungary, we spent many memorable and meaningful holidays with our grandchildren (a trip to Cape Cod in the summer of 2014 particularly sticks in our minds), strengthening our bonds and encouraging them to learn from the world around them the values we hold dear—curiosity, inclusiveness, authenticity, and generosity.

* * *

Alan's retirement from education in June 2016 marked a turning point in our married life.

This newfound freedom allowed us to visit our three children and our grandchildren on a more regular basis, and to experience even more travel and life adventures.

This, in turn, enabled me to express and develop my authentic self even further.

In July 2017, we were fortunate to be able to take a trip to the Abruzzo region of Central Italy. At a silent auction, our daughter Alanis won a one-week stay at a villa near Cassino, which she kindly offered to us. The villa could host up to twelve people.

Originally, we were hoping to share this amazing opportunity with our son Chad, his two teenage sons, and two of their friends. About two months before the date, our son informed us that he would be unable to honour the invitation, as his boys now had summer jobs. This was disappointing, of course, but understandable.

We decided to share the holiday with two former students I had taught in 1979 in Germany, one of whom now had a family. Rounding out the guest list was a life coach who, years before, had taken my after-school yoga classes for teachers, and who eventually asked me if I would give her some private "life coaching" sessions. She joined us with her daughter and her Italian husband, who offered to extend our time in Italy by staying at his family residence in a small town called Roccomontepiano.

That made eleven of us; we were good to go for an entire week of amazing communal living.

Everyone got along fabulously and pitched in with the cooking and the planning of memorable outings. These included the Amalfi Coast, with such storied locations as Capri, Sorrento, Pompeii, and Mount Vesuvius. We were very fortunate to get a private excursion to the Isle of Capri, which included a meal on the boat, a variety of drinks, as well as a swim in the famous Blue Grotto. It was magical!

As we readied to leave, our captain Roberto pulled up the buoys with the boat already in motion, I jumped up to steer our boat and prevent a mishap, as there were several small boats about. Roberto was so grateful for this unexpected assistance that he "fell in love" with me from that moment on. He was the age of my oldest son Chad and happily married, but boy did he ever carry on... He even had help from my own husband! Alan shared with Roberto that, in our previous trips to Italy, I always commented that the reputation Italian men had of pinching a lady's bum was unfounded, since it had never happened to me. So Alan asked him to pinch my bottom, and Roberto happily complied. To this day, Alan and I reminisce and relive the moment.

10.4. Italy, 2017.
Source: Family Collection.

At the end of the week, we extended our stay in Italy and had daily excursions and adventures. Alan had heard about a couple from Ottawa who had sold everything and moved to Torre de' Passeri to start a tourist villa. He was impressed with their risk taking and their courage to leave Canada permanently to set up a home and business in the Abruzzo region of Italy and wanted to meet them and find out more about them. He found their contact information and arranged for us to drive there to check it out. When we arrived, Lisa and Jake welcomed us with open arms: cappuccino, a guided tour, introduction to the staff, relaxing time by the pool, and a delicious snack.

The friendship formed and for our last night in Italy we booked with them as paying guests. We were so impressed by all the care and attention to detail; it is no wonder their business is thriving. We stayed in touch once we returned home. They even came for a meal here with us in Ottawa and invited us years later to a customer appreciation event they hosted.

⋆ ⋆ ⋆

10.5. – 10.7. Blue Grotto, Capri, 2017.
Source: Family Collection.

One of my favourite sayings is "Bloom where you are planted."

We certainly did that over the next three years leading up to that nefarious pandemic. When Alan first asked me to go on a cruise, my response was nasty: "I'd rather eat glass and die." His persistence convinced me to go, not just once, but five times in all so far.

We saw these cruises as opportunities to learn new things and meet new people. We discovered a new musical genre thanks to my stepfather, Eloi McCully, when we took him on a Big Band-themed Mexican Riviera cruise in 2008. On another, we met the talented English violinist Chris Watkins. We bought his CD at the time and have kept in touch ever since. One cruise brought us to the Caribbean island of Saint Lucia in February 2020. To our delight, the family members of our live-in babysitter from the late 1970s and early 1980s in Ottawa greeted us as if we were family and guided us to the highlights of their island. Even though the babysitting days were decades away, we still kept in touch to share special times or special memories.

We never forget the people who have had an impact on our lives or on those of our children.

What was peculiar about this particular cruise, which started on the last week of January 2020, was its timing. We kept hearing announcements indicating an overload in the sick bay of the ship or stating new rules and regulations that we had never experienced before on any of our previous cruises. For instance, we were to sit at separate tables without other passengers. We could not reach in for our favourite fruit but had to ask for it to be handed over on our plates. Each time we entered the dining area, we were told to use sanitizer on our hands. When we arrived at our final destination in Fort Lauderdale, Florida, we were still wondering why we had to observe so many preventive health precautions. That is when we understood we had just experienced the first hints of the oncoming global pandemic.

* * *

With COVID, it felt like the shades were being drawn on the sun and the entire world.

All the exciting events that had been part of our regular lives suddenly came to a standstill. My extroverted side was shutting down again. No longer able to travel to new places and long-distance locations, I literally felt deprived of a source of oxygen. If we wanted to see people—and I need to see people—we were restricted to al fresco visits in backyard patios. Eventually, even that was limited to a single core group of six people. For someone like me, that seriously impeded my personal development.

The pandemic also interrupted my desire to help seniors via my chair yoga classes. I was told not to come in person but to teach classes on Zoom. For me, that meant no music, which is a highlight of the classes I teach, as it motivates

10.8. With stepfather Eloi McCully, 2008.
Source: Family Collection.

and enhances the movements for all the participants. Teaching Zoom classes for me was a major punishment. When I was finally allowed to go in person, I had to do a COVID test. This meant doing a nasal test and waiting fifteen minutes to get the results indicating I was negative. In one of the locations where I taught, they gave me a certificate stating that I tested negative in the morning. Upon arriving at my next class, they would not accept the certificate, and I had to go through the whole testing procedure again.

I am so grateful that I believe in perseverance; otherwise, I would have quit my chair yoga business. Throughout all this, I tried to look on the bright side of life and apply what my mother had taught me long ago: "What is the gift in any negative situation?"

I searched for the positive in all the sanitary restrictions and realized that we did develop a greater awareness of personal health and protection, self-care and mental health, exercise, nutrition, and meditation.

But I also tried to be a positive force in the world. With COVID, morale was waning for so many of us that I began to make collages of positive messages and would hand those out on little pieces of paper to anyone who made eye contact, smiled, or communicated with me. Alan called this a random act of kindness.

I shared over seven hundred of these little notes during these years. The responses I most often got were: "Oh, you so made my day," or "I needed this to help me cope," or "I have a bulletin board at home of the ones you have given me."

11 Looking Back: A Unique Life Story

As I look in the rearview mirror, I have a chance to contemplate and ponder what my life journey was all about and where it has brought me. Leaving everything I loved behind and rushing to exit Hungary in such stressful circumstances and in such a state of massive confusion, caused an underlying sadness, which I never had time to really express or fully come to terms with. For the child that I was, such a brutal rupture, which started with escaping the "bad guys" in Hungary and finished with our arrival in a foreign land where I did not speak the language, produced feelings of abandonment and bewilderment, which simply overwhelmed me. The reality of life at that time made me retreat and withdraw from the confident, outgoing, and sociable self I had been up to that point. I needed to make sense of my new life. In the years that followed, I came to understand that I possessed the inner strength and tenacity to keep learning and to always persevere.

But I could not have done it alone. I am very grateful to all my family members, friends, and even strangers who have enriched my life along the way and helped me to identify and reclaim my true, authentic self. Both the traumatic and the joyful experiences I have lived have shaped me into a loving, giving, and compassionate person, which I believe has always been my profound nature.

In my eyes, the eighty-year-old woman I am now is fundamentally the same as the ten-year-old girl who escaped Communism in the 1950s; I still like to laugh, play, exercise, share, help out, meet new people, and make new friends. I feel that my transformation back to who I really am was a liberation from former thoughts, beliefs, behaviours, and definitely cycles of suffering. To cleanse my feelings of separation from my homeland, I returned to Hungary on more than one occasion, either with my husband Alan and our own family, or with my mother and sister, or all of us together. One time in Budapest, as we were walking along the Danube near the Parliament building, we saw in the distance some iron shoes cemented on the pavement. As we got closer, we realized that this was a memorial for the Jewish people arrested during the Nazi occupation, who had been ordered to take off their shoes (a valuable item at the time), then tied together and shot at the edge of the water so that their bodies fell into the river. The memorial represented their shoes left behind on the bank. That was an incredibly moving moment, which made the atrocities committed in my native city during the Second World War very real for us.

Although as an immigrant, I was always taught to forget my origins and assimilate into Canadian society, I am glad to see that, as they get older, my own children have developed a certain curiosity and even pride in their family roots, both Jewish and Hungarian. Our son Wade has expressed a desire to get a Hungarian passport, and our daughter Alanis was featured in an episode of the PBS series "Finding Your Roots," which focused on her Jewish ancestry.

What pleases me even more is to see that this interest seems to have been passed on to the next generation. When our eldest grandson was in Europe, on a college exchange, he made an effort to go to Budapest to experience his Hungarian heritage. While there, he visited my childhood home and FaceTimed us as he was standing in front of the apartment and showed us the latest renovations to the building, which now covered the wartime bullet holes in the bricks. For me, this was another unforgettable connection with my grandson and with my past that came together in this very special place.

All these memories from family trips welled up in me and inspired me to write my story in the hope that it might give others the impetus to reflect on their life's legacy and the impact it has on those who are close to them.

⋆ ⋆ ⋆

Over the course of my life, I have had to overcome a number of psychological hurdles, many of which came from a lack of self-confidence as an immigrant woman, to be able to let my authentic self shine through.

I believe that being aware of these (often self-imposed) preconceptions or limitations can help all those who, like me, have struggled or are still struggling with similar issues on their path to personal growth and evolution.

Throughout the experiences, adventures, and travels that have forced me out of my comfort zone but that have, at the same time, allowed me to find myself again and regain confidence, I have learned not to "dim" myself anymore, not to conceal my attributes or my talents, not to hide behind a mask to protect my vulnerability.

I no longer feel I am not enough.

I no longer wonder how I should present myself to others, how others will perceive me, or if it is even safe to be myself with others.

I no longer fear that people will see me for who I am.

I no longer seek their approval or live wanting to be accepted and not simply ignored.

I no longer put myself down. "Playing small" no longer serves me.

11.1. The old apartment, Budapest, early 2000s.
Source: Family Collection.

Instead of focusing on what I am not, I have chosen to assert myself and focus on what I am. I dare to ask for what I want, what I need, what I deserve. I am my own best friend. I have let go of expectations and have given myself more space to grow and to manifest more positively. I have accepted the fact that I am still and always will be evolving.

To help me achieve these aspirational goals, I have come to rely on a series of impactful thoughts or sayings that have often guided my life decisions. I regularly share them in my yoga classes or training sessions and have mentioned them throughout these memoirs.

I believe that "Whenever it's possible to say yes, say yes." We each have a comfort zone and if we do the same thing over and over, it begins to shrink. To expand it, it is important to step out and try new things or tackle new ideas. Naturally, the

11.2. Georgia, her mother, and sister, Kati, at the airport, Budapest, early 2000s.
Source: Family Collection.

logical conclusion of this is: "Try it, you might like it." You can never know if you like something or not unless and until you give it a chance.

A senior group once asked me to join in on a laughter yoga class, and although I was not particularly enthusiastic about the concept, I accepted the invitation and attended. I ended up learning that your body does not know if your laughter is real or not and therefore you can trick it into feeling good. Now I can pretend-laugh, and it has indeed changed my mood for the better.

But in order for something like this to work or to have a real and lasting impact on your life, you must "Use it or lose it." A person must identify what actions truly benefit their wellness and well-being by practising them regularly, so as not to lose the positive effects of this routine.

My mother always used to say: "Look for the gift in any life situation." This saying has helped me cope and understand why things happen, whether positive or negative. Because of this, I have always deemed it important to "Count your blessings, not your missings." Instead of dwelling on the negative, you should concentrate on the positive, focus on what you already have rather than on what is missing in your life.

I have found a similar saying useful when a seemingly overwhelming task looms ahead: "An elephant is eaten one bite at a time." I take it to mean, be happy with what you have achieved so far and keep moving forward consistently.

As another saying goes: "Quitters never win, and winners never quit."

* * *

11.3. Sculpture, Shoes on the Danube Bank, Budapest, early 2000s.
Source: Family Collection.

My favourite bird is the hummingbird. It stops before deciding which way to go. It teaches me to stop and think before acting or reacting.

Similarly, I ask myself, "And then what?" whenever I face adversity or rejection. It helps put things in perspective.

This happened when I printed off and cut out small sayings to hand out to people during the pandemic to help uplift their spirits. One day, after handing out several hundreds, for which I consistently received heartfelt appreciation, a cashier gazed at the one I offered her and threw it in the garbage. I stood there for a second, mouth agape. I then consciously chose not to respond negatively; I refused to "give my power away."

This recalls one of the most powerful mindsets I know, and which brings me great strength and comfort: "Some will. Some won't. So what! Someone's waiting!" In other words, do not give up too easily and do not let the naysayers affect you. There are always other options and other people around the corner.

I try to apply such a positive approach to all my relationships. When talking or dealing with someone, I always ask myself: "Will this response be a win-win?" Will my words have a positive impact on both of us? If not, then I prefer not to say anything.

This should lead us to value and seek compromise in all our personal interactions. Before agreeing or refusing to do something, I believe it is important to honestly evaluate (on a scale of 1 to 10, for instance) and discuss how much you and the person asking each want to do that thing. For two people to be really connected, both need to feel "seen, safe, and heard" by the other. If that is not there, then it is not a deep friendship.

Since many of my close friends feel safe sharing their issues with me, it can sometimes get overwhelming.

To protect myself, I have lived by the following words: "I didn't cause it, I don't own it, I won't hold it." This does not mean that I do not care. I am still happy to listen and to help, but I have my own issues to deal with and cannot take on someone else's as well. I simply cannot pile your story onto mine.

* * *

Sayings and empowering statements speak to the perseverance and resilience required to go through life.

For me, they serve as powerful reminders that confidence, compassion, and positivity need to be constantly cultivated if we want them to grow in ourselves and in our world.

This is what this book is all about, really. Building on years of sharing small tokens of positivity with the people who cross my path, I have intertwined these adages into my own personal history in the hopes that my story serves as an example of gratitude and might, in some small way, create a ripple of positive change in the world.

In a way, my book is a longer, more elaborate version of my gratitude stones and motivational messages. My stories and my messages are one... together, they weave a story of love. Of love for my husband and gratitude for the rich, fanciful, adventurous life we have had and continue to lead, for the hard times that allowed us to grow, for our cherished children and grandchildren, who endlessly enchant us as we watch them pursue their own journey, for our wonderful extended family and the delightful friends we have made along our own journey.

I was forced to flee a violent revolution in my homeland. My new life was not always easy. But I chose gratitude over resentment; evolution over power and bitterness. Alacrity is my credo, and gratitude my revolution.

And this, my friends, is what I humbly offer.

Beyond the Narrative

About Georgia: Reflections from Family, Friends, and Colleagues

Testimonials and memories from some people who crossed paths with Georgia and who are feeling the "Georgia Love."

Children

I JUST WANTED to tell you guys that you are an amazing set of parents. I'm very grateful for both of you and grateful for all the things you did for me. How much you believe in me and how much self-confidence I've developed largely because of you two as my mom and dad. I love you both.

Chad Morissette

DEAR MOM, I hope you know you are the most wonderful woman in this world. And even though it may seem like I'm breaking free, I'll never really break away. Because our love is always there. Thanks for understanding and being so beautiful (inside and out). You deserve happiness and every good thing that's happening to you. I love you.

Alanis Morissette

TO BE MARRIED for so many years is extraordinary. An accomplishment that is not easily attained, especially in this era. Mom and Dad, during the past years, I have witnessed many things that have enriched my life and I'm sure many others.

You have understood each other, have compromised when conflict and different opinions arose, have listened, and have changed for the better and for the growth of your relationship. You have shown strength and security, two qualities that demand more than you can imagine. You have travelled together, seen half the world together, have tasted many of life's experiences. You both seem to have an impenetrable bond. A tie that I have never seen anyone else in the world achieve. Moments like this are too often overlooked. I have great admiration for your marriage. The love you both have has made me thankful. The most important quality I've seen you share is your openness of communication and affection. You are both great examples of what a marriage should contain. It is these attributes that have kept you happy and fulfilled, and it's these qualities that are being passed on to your children and the generations to come.

A reflection on the past and what has been achieved in the present symbolizes another chapter of successful companionship, a sustaining friendship. You've managed to keep the romance alive through numerous stages of your marriage, from a husband and wife to parenthood, from career changes to your new ambitions and interests. I love you both.

Wade Imre Morissette

Grandchildren

Extraordinary Person

IMAGINE SOMEONE IS ten years old and they must escape the country that they have lived in for all their life and start over in a new place.

To be able to experience this and still grow up, and have an amazing personality, and to live with such positivity means you must be extraordinary. My grandmother is an extraordinary person because she is courageous. She showed this character trait when she had to escape from Hungary. She's also extremely loving and super silly. Every time she visits, she always brings us toys or a gift card. She also sends us loving texts and quotes. And every time we see her, she greets us with a very big hug.

Georgia does lots of silly things. That's why I like to joke that she is immature, and she is always trying to prove that statement right (surprisingly). One time when we were walking in Stanley Park, she started to play the song "Cha Cha Slide" and began dancing to the song. I was about seven years old then, so when I saw my *Nagyi* ("grandma" in Hungarian) dancing to a really fun song in public, I thought it was hysterical but also a bit embarrassing. Extraordinary people are rare and if someone has an extraordinary person like her in their life, they should appreciate them.

Finn Morissette

I'VE ALWAYS LOOKED up to my grandma (*Nagyi* as we call her). She is the kindest human I've ever met. Whether it be the beautiful meditations she sends to her grandkids or the slips of paper with quotes that she hands out to strangers she meets. I find her kindness infectious, making me a more caring and compassionate person. A great example of this was when she came to support my Ultimate team. She gave each of my teammates a slip of paper with an inspiring message on it. She also recognized that one of them was going through a hard time and supported her. Months afterwards, my teammates still hold onto these pieces of paper.

Seeing the impact she had with something relatively small and simple inspired me. I started sending daily positive quotes to all of my close friends. I also began to make public pieces of art with quotes to motivate people and spread good vibes. I would never have started this without her initial acts of kindness and seeing how much people appreciated them. Her unwavering positivity and love for people—regardless of who they are—makes this world a better place. Because of her, I will always continue to look for the silver lining and find beauty in every aspect of life. I love you, *Nagyi*.

Beck Morissette

NAGYI HAS HAD a major impact on my life in many ways, and I can't thank her enough for helping raise me when I was little, and for being the best grandma ever. Over the years, *Nagyi* has taught me countless things, but there are three life lessons that will always remind me of her. First, *Nagyi* showed me each and every day the importance of being kind to others. I have never seen anyone hand out so many little papers to strangers, but that idea of spreading happiness was what made *Nagyi* one of a kind. Second, she taught me the importance of always finding a way to laugh and have fun at everything you do. It didn't matter whether it was at work, school, or home, *Nagyi* always told me: "You better be laughing or you're in the wrong situation." Lastly, I really admire *Nagyi's* motivation to continue teaching yoga to this day. She taught me the importance of staying active your whole life and to strive to find a job that you enjoy doing at any age.

I love you, *Nagyi*! Can't wait for the next toffee pull!

Noah Faulkner-Morissette

NAGYI HAS BEEN a constant source of love, strength, and support throughout my life, acting as a second mother to my brother and me. From the time when we were little, she was always there, travelling with us, cheering us on, and ensuring we had every opportunity to pursue our dreams. She never hesitated to step in and help our parents, whether lending a hand during busy times or simply bringing joy and laughter into our lives. Beyond supporting us, *Nagyi* is the rock that holds our family together. Her steady presence, wisdom, and kindness always create a sense of unity that keeps us all connected, no matter where life takes us. She makes everyone around her feel unique, always offering a warm smile, a listening ear, or a comforting word. Even now, she continues to be an important role model in my life, teaching me the value of resilience, love, and selflessness. *Nagyi's* ability to spread joy and unite people is truly a gift, and her impact on our family is immeasurable. Love you *Nagyi*!

Caleb Faulkner-Morissette

I ENJOYED SPENDING the holidays with you and all the toffee pulls. I am excited to read your book.

Ever Treadway

Extended Family

AS GEORGIA'S YOUNGER sister, I know her life inside and out and have witnessed her become all that she is. As she discloses her personal journey from Hungary to Canada through her perspective and experiences, she delivers her life story transparently. Life has moulded her, sculpted her, and made her the loving presence that she is to all those whose lives she so caringly touches. If you are reading these pages, you are woven into a tapestry of her struggles and triumphs, and may emerge a better version of yourself in what it reveals to you about who you are. May your voyage through each page illuminate your own blessings and inspire you to embrace the gift that you are to humanity.

Kati Alexandra

KNOWING GEORGIA, OUR sister-in-law, for over half a century, we believe her motto is "live, love, laugh, and laugh more."

We love you.

Rick and Sue Morissette

I WILL BE forever grateful that my life path has intersected with Georgia's. Knowing her journey, starting from so far away, and how the Universe aligned to ensure that she showed up as the gift she is in my life, was truly divine intervention. Her impact on me, and the woman I have become, is so woven into my life that I cannot imagine it without her or her influence. She has been a source of maternal love from the very first time she asked the young university student sitting in her kitchen what was on my heart. She helped me navigate so many phases and changes in my life, get through some of the happiest, challenging, and darkest days as an adult, that I honestly don't know how I would have done it without her. She is a constant source of love, support, laughter, late night talks, tears, hugs (the best hugs), travel companionship (but don't try going through security with her), and the recipient of my middle of the night phone calls.

Georgia is love in action, mother, sister, wife, friend, and the best *Nagyi* ever. Love cannot express the depth of emotions that our bond shares. Forever, my mother-in-love.

Bobbi Faulkner

Friends

Every day is a journey, a fresh chance to grow
Motions to heal our bodies, poses to enhance our glow
Self-improvement she lives by, and forever sets the tone
Sharing her experiences with others, lest they feel alone
Her pride is the senior classes, of which she often speaks
Ever ready to try a new move, despite their assorted squeaks
She hosts many workshops, where transformations take place
Opportunities to awaken, and discover inner grace
The words powerful and patient, describe my Yogi well
(it's fairly obvious here, but I think she's really swell)
Mindful of movement, attentive to rainbows nearby
Cheering those around her, to reach for the sky
With ever heartening messages, hard to dismiss
All aspects of being, are hard for a chance at true bliss
Her yoga classes inspire, those who attend
Forever a new beginning, by no means an end
Thus, so I write, to exclaim big and loud
That this lovely lady, has good reason to be proud
She's modest and nurturing, caring and kind
It's my blessed luck to have made this sunny yoga find
Let butterflies and ladybugs release us, beauty to behold
Encouraged by those around us, precious as pure gold
Loyal and loving, stirring others to stand tall
Proud to call her Yogi, but friend most of all.

Paula Cote

GEORGIA WALKED INTO my life in 1979. It was the first day of school in late August of my Grade 7 year and I was eleven years old. We were children of Canadian Forces personnel who lived in Lahr, West Germany (at the time), and we shared a profound bond that is referred to as being Army brats.

I will never forget the anticipation on that first day, riding on the green school bus. All my friends were loudly chatting about their summer holiday. I was very distracted and did not eagerly participate in the conversation. I was solely thinking about one thing: "Would I be so lucky to get Mrs. Morissette this year?" Mrs. Morissette's reputation as a great teacher had built up over the previous two years, I only wanted her as my teacher. I remember the immeasurable excitement when I found out she was indeed my teacher, and when I walked through the door of her classroom for the very first time. It was the best first day of school EVER. That was the day my life literally changed forever.

We were blessed in Lahr to be taught by the best of the best. The recruiting process for overseas teachers was highly competitive. Often, they chose principals and vice-principals to fill teaching roles in Canadian Forces schools.

I learned so many life lessons in Georgia's class. I call these "Georgia-isms": character, accountability, humility, humanity. Her pedagogical style was years ahead of her time. Back in the day, when students were still sitting in rows, or teachers presenting a very stern side of their personality to instill effective classroom management, Georgia embraced flexible seating. Her smile cast a magic spell on us all, and we didn't dare misbehave in her class. Disappointing her would have broken our hearts! We strove to be our best selves because we all loved her so much. How lucky we were. She really taught us to take responsibility for our own actions. I never experienced a school year that could offer me so much happiness and sense of belonging as my Grade 7 year. Georgia was simply my favourite, and that still stands to this day.

She regaled us with the incredible story of her family's escape from Hungary in 1956 when she was just a child. We were mesmerized. We begged to stay in at breaks so we could hear more. I will never forget how impactful her story was. I was only two or three years older than she was at the time of the escape. I thought of her for years to come, and when in bookstores, I always looked for "the book" that she had hoped to write someday. Despite all that Georgia has endured, she is literally the most positive person I have ever met. She touches every soul she sees. She is pure love.

I was incredibly blessed to come back into Georgia's life again in 2009, twenty-nine years after I stood before her on the last day of school, holding back the tears as I said goodbye. I could not believe my good fortune when, after reaching out to her, she agreed to see me. Our reunion was wonderful.

As the years went by, my own family grew to love her as much as I do. She is a constant source of sage advice and offers it with the utmost love and understanding. Whenever I experience a low moment, I think to myself that I could use some "Georgia Love." Everyone should know the feeling of Georgia love. It's the best.

Laura Morrison

I MET GEORGIA in 1968, one year after I emigrated to Canada from my homeland of Wales, UK. I was a professional singer performing in Hull, Quebec. We instinctively became best friends. We have shared a friendship that spans over fifty years.

We were young and excited about life. Georgia was so vibrant but was kind of shy to be her real self. It was as if she was breaking out of a shell. When I first met her, she was hesitant to wear new things including 60s fashion, which I was very excited about. One day when we went shopping, she tried on a hat which was puffy at the crown and had a peak at the front. A bit like what Bob Dylan would wear... really 60s! It looked great on her and she actually bought it. It seemed to be the start of her shedding her skin and letting go of the old to bring in the new.

Being a schoolteacher, Georgia also became interested in teaching yoga. I love her yoga lessons just as much as her Hungarian cooking! She combines skill, talent, and personality with a non-judgmental mentoring style and a generous heart. We used to love to crochet and just talk about life. It was, and still is an honest, true conversation, whether serious or full of laughs. Never a dull moment. Yet what we've had is a deep, trusting friendship then, and still now, because... what you see is what you get!

Georgia has given so much more than she could ever receive in life. She has been strong, kind, and brave enough to overcome the shattering fears she endured in her past Hungarian experience when she had to flee for her life.

I can say that she is the most beautiful woman inside and out and I am privileged to call her my friend.

Jacquie Morgan

THANK YOU BOTH so much for our beautiful friendship! We were fortunate to meet Georgia and Alan twelve years ago, at a community event just after we moved to Ottawa from London, Ontario.

Georgia immediately made our family feel welcome, and we found we had so much in common. Our friendship blossomed with her kindness and generosity, and her philosophy to "Count our blessings, not our missings!"

Georgia is a sought-after and amazing yoga instructor; among her clients are retirement homes and senior residences in Ottawa, where her vibrancy and colourful style are welcomed by all. Georgia is surely one of the most positive people you will ever meet and an inspiration for us all.

Susan Laneville

I CAN SEE why Georgia's daughter is so successful today. I received a pinch of what she received her whole life, one day sitting at the kitchen table having tea with Georgia.

Georgia was one of the first persons to instill self-confidence in me. I still have the little elephant pin she gave me twenty-five years ago. She said: "Think of this elephant as an example of your life, it's big and you need to take little bites at a time. You got this." These words were said with so much love and encouragement they propelled me towards a journey in finding myself and who I am today.

Thank you, Georgia. You changed more lives than you know.

Josee Madison

I DON'T REMEMBER the exact circumstances in which I first met Georgia. I do remember that she told me she was the neighbourhood yenta. Not a gossipy or nosy yenta, but rather a source of news and goings-on in the community. More like a town crier. It turns out she is neither. She's actually a first responder. When tragedy struck our family, it was Georgia who ran head first into the flames while family and friends receded. She volunteered her skills as a yoga instructor week after week providing both physical therapy and humour. The yoga sessions have stopped, but she's always available for an injection of kindness and laughter whenever we're in need.

Steve Baumann

GEORGIA AND I first met in grade school some sixty-five years ago. She was a soft-spoken, shy student, who unbeknownst to many of her fellow classmates, had already suffered unknown and devastating hardships in her young life. Through it all, she always had a smile on her beautiful face, a kind word to share, and always led by positive example. All these many years later, she continues to empower her family, friends, and students to be their most joyful, bold, and authentic self, and by doing so they inspire others. With love and admiration.

Yvette Wu

I HAVE KNOWN Georgia for quite some time now. I have never met anyone so caring and loving in all my life. I've been going to yoga classes with Georgia and enjoying every minute of it. We walk into a retirement home and she revives everyone there. Why can't there be more people like her in this world? Georgia is a remarkable lady. I have had a tremendous number of friends in my life, but I have to say she has been my best friend ever. All my love to you, Georgia, and the wonderful man you married Alan.

Denise Seguin

I'M BOTH PLEASED and proud to say I have known Georgia since 1977 and, as a young child would say, she was a mentor to me. We met on the Canadian Forces base in Lahr, as she and her wonderful husband, Alan, were both hired as teachers in the base like my dad. In fact, we had already been living in a nearby village for a year when we were first introduced to the Morissette family. Assigned to be their sponsor family, they moved into our place, and we moved closer to the base. Our families hit it off immediately, as we all shared a passion for adventure, our pursuit of education and a taste for fun!

I developed a close relationship with the Morissette family as their regular babysitter and even played Mr. Mom for a week when Georgia was away supervising a school trip. She and Alan are wonderful parents and built a home where love and respect were evident. Friends felt at once part of their family and were honoured and made to feel at home. Georgia likes to laugh, even at her own expense. She's transparent in the very best sense. Fun defines my friend, Georgia. I would also say she has a kind and generous heart. It is no surprise to me that her songwriter daughter penned a song in her mom's honour and aptly called it "*Heart of the House*". My friendship with her (and her whole clan) continued and deepened over the years. As a student at Laval University in Québec City for several years, I would often visit them in Ottawa. Ever the educator, Georgia would take me on tours in the areas she knew that I would find interesting.

I currently run music therapy sessions with youngsters with developmental disabilities. When Georgia and Alan were visiting me recently, I invited them to attend a session. The kids responded favourably to Georgia's engagement with them, and they basked in the warmth of her infectious smile. As we left the session, I asked her about the noticeably positive reaction, to which she replied: "Throughout the entire singsong, I was quietly performing healing Reiki on those beautiful children." It was for me an unforgettable moment and the perfect illustration of the depth of Georgia's compassion, kindness, and generosity. She always has and always will touch hearts wherever she goes.

Georgia embodies the multicultural ideal to which Canadians hold dearly and is understandably proud of her Hungarian origins. She's interested in others and what makes them tick. She is always genuine and straightforward.

Cam Culham

GEORGIA, YOU SAID, "And then what?" Those words have changed my perspective. My wonderful friend, I liked you from the very moment we met. Of course, we have a lot in common, especially our love of our families, children, and grandchildren. Over the years, we have become more like sisters going for walks, talking, and sometimes even practising yoga.

I love you for your enthusiasm, zest for life, and gift of storytelling. Fleeing Hungary, coming to Canada, having a happy marriage, living in Germany, raising children, teaching in school, getting the white Topaz, and developing a yoga practice in your fifties, are but a few examples that inspire me. I can't wait to see what's next.

Sherri Ryan

GEORGIA AND I have been friends for over forty years. Our relationship is so special that I'm honoured to share my feelings and thoughts about this incredible woman. Georgia brings joy to everyone she meets. She's loving, has a great sense of humour, and I marvel at her ability to care for the seniors to whom she teaches yoga. She embraces each person and makes them feel appreciated and respected. At the end of each class, Georgia goes to each person and gets their permission to massage their shoulders and gives them words of encouragement for their efforts. This woman is to be admired and appreciated for all the joy that she brings to each one of these seniors.

In all the years I have known Georgia, she never really shared the incredible story of her escape to Canada. She did share some small tidbits about her parents and her sibling's feelings towards Communism. When I heard the complete history of her family's journey and how terrifying it was to escape from Hungary, I was in total shock. After learning about her background and how she was sworn to secrecy about her Jewish heritage, my total admiration for this dear friend grew even more. Can you just imagine how difficult it must have been for a twelve-year-old to hold this secret? I know that through all this adversity, hardship, pain, and fear that Georgia faced, she chose not to let this painful past define her and rob her of an incredible life.

Georgia met her true love in public school, a relationship that is so special and so deep that it has been ongoing for over sixty-five years. Georgia and Alan have raised three incredible children, and have the joy of seeing each one of them succeed in their own lives. And now enjoy the gift of grandchildren, who only add to the joy Georgia and Alan share together.

Joan Olinik

GEORGIA MORISSETTE TEACHES yoga to seniors in Ottawa, Canada. Almost eighty herself, she started to learn yoga after the age of fifty when chronic back pain was impacting the quality of her life. Having spent her career as a schoolteacher, Georgia understands how people learn, and how she needs to modify her strategy to reach different students, something she brings to her yoga teaching. Having experienced firsthand the life-altering impact of regular yoga practice, she began to teach senior citizens, most of whom have never practiced yoga, and may not have even been very active throughout their life. I'm very happy to have her as a guest on the podcast to discuss the skills and strategies needed to teach and to learn yoga at any age, as well as to share her many wonderful tips for well-being throughout life.

Kinga Petrovai

LIFELONG FRIEND IS not a throwaway term; it is earned. Earned from a lifetime of shared experiences between two friends not just when times are happy and shiny, but also when you need that one person you know will be there for you when you are at your lowest point. For me, that person has always been Georgia. I still remember that smiling face walking into our first class together in elementary school. She did not speak a word of English, but you could just feel her positivity and genuineness. We became friends.

I always felt a sense of comfort around her, even at that young age. Not surprisingly, Georgia learned English quickly and, by year's end, was, in fact, a top student. Her family was my family. I would be remiss if I did not mention the wonderful times we had with Georgia's mom and grandmother. Such gentle and loving people. No doubt this is where Georgia developed her loving spirit. It's funny how life takes you from sharing Malted Milk chocolates walking home from Immaculata High School, to having that same friend hold your hand and support you when there are the inevitable losses and challenges in your life.

Even though I do not see her every day, I know that she will be that person I can rely on for unconditional support. We have different personalities, but perhaps that is why we have worked so well all these years. A true sense of comfort with an old friend. When you are with Georgia, you always laugh. How lucky am I to call her my lifelong friend.

Gail Thompson

THE UNIVERSE CONNECTED us at just the right time. I give you my deeply felt gratitude. Thank you for the absolute light and love you bring to my life. Your kindness, although it may seem like a small gesture, has far-reaching impacts on me; on my mind, my body, and my soul. You have helped me to come out of my comfort zone, to reach deep inside myself and pull out the confidence I need to exude more often. You bring me a sense of inner balance that helps shift my energy towards healing and self-care. You motivate me to take better care of this life vessel we call our body. You are unique and such a beautiful down-to-earth soul. The world needs more of you. I will pass along to others the love, laughter, and light I feel around you.

Namaste. May you honour the light within you.

Brandie Young

MY BEST FRIENDS Alan and Georgia have made every day knowing them brighter. They are a listening ear and with their encouraging words, have helped me navigate through a challenging time, on more than one occasion. Georgia has the incredible ability to connect with anyone. I've watched her walk up to a stranger and hand them a note with words of positivity. I've watched her instantly lift their spirits and bring a smile to their face. With his contagious enthusiasm, Alan can bring so many creative ideas to any situation, and make you feel like you can achieve anything. Now, they have shared their memoirs in this book with such honesty and depth that it completely drew me in from the first page. They have lived an extraordinary life, and this book is a testament to their courage, dedication, passion, and love. It's a must read!

Darlene Morgan

I MET GEORGIA in 1957 when she was brought into my class at Saint Aloysius School in Ottawa, after escaping the Soviets in Hungary in 1956. She spoke no English and was a very shy little girl. I remember that she always had the most beautiful smile and a twinkle in her eyes. We became friends immediately.

She was a fast learner and mastered English very quickly. She was also very smart. She was the best at math in our class. She lived very close to where my family lived, and loved coming over to our house filled with noise and many children. I remember going to her apartment on Wurtemburg Street for the first time and being shocked. It had no furniture and very little of anything, but they seemed so happy and grateful to be in Ottawa. I also remember she and her sister had no toys. She told me they had escaped and couldn't even bring their dolls.

To this day, sixty-nine years later, I consider her to be one of my most valued friends. Even though we don't see each other very often, I know I can pick up the phone and pick up the conversation where we left off the last time. She is one of the kindest, warmest women, I know.

Colleen Hooper

I HAD RECENTLY moved to the Ottawa area with my family and had just started a new teaching position. It was stressful, as teaching can be in a new school, and on top of that I had just learned that my mother was diagnosed with a terminal form of cancer. I decided to sign up for a yoga class that took place after school in the hope that it would help me through all the chaos that had surrounded me. So, I attended Georgia's yoga class. She immediately introduced herself, welcomed me, and said that it was nice to meet me. She was so calming and soothing. I knew this art form was exactly what I needed. What I didn't know was that she would become so very dear to me and my family going forward.

It wasn't long before Georgia and I started developing a strong friendship. It was easy since we enjoyed many of the same activities. We both loved treasure hunting and second-hand clothing, sales, yoga, and paddle boarding, to name but a few things. Wherever we went, time would fly by and we would talk for hours! When I say the Morissettes became like family, I really am not kidding! As my children grew up, the two families grew together. Soon my kids and I began attending Georgia's yoga classes in her home where we also had the pleasure of getting to know Alan better. Then Georgia was invited to my daughter's wedding shower. Naturally, she and Alan came to her wedding, and then, of course, to the baby shower! She even allowed my grandson to come to a yoga class and demon-strate how to do a downward dog at nine months of age! The truth is, Georgia and Alan changed my life and that of my family. They guided me and those nearest and dearest to me through difficult times, sharing as well many joyful family memories. They are now and always will be a very treasured part of my life.

Darlene Morrow

THE MOMENT I met Georgia, I knew we'd be kindred spirits. She has an innate ability to make you feel instantly comfortable; as if you've known each other for years! Georgia exudes positivity. She often jokes, albeit truthfully, that she is a nauseatingly positive person, but I think we all need a little more positivity in our lives. If you are lucky enough to have the opportunity to meet Georgia, you will instantly be given a little cut-out piece of paper, with an anecdote or lyric exuding positivity, girl power, or self-care. I remember one time driving home from work. I came to a four-way stop. The driver with the right of way proceeded through the intersection. As I was preparing to drive forward, the next car to my right decided to follow the previous driver and continue through the intersection. I was so mad! I honked my horn, gave an unpleasant hand gesture, then stopped. I took a few deep breaths and said to myself: "What would Georgia do? How would Georgia react in this situation?" Georgia would say: "...and then what? How does getting upset help me? It doesn't make me feel good." So, for the rest of my drive home, I smiled and thought only positive thoughts. Because that's what Georgia would do.

Kelly Blackburn

DEAR GEORGIA, I have known you since 1997. Our friendship has evolved over the years to the point that I now consider you like a soul sister. Your warm smile lights up the room and fills up the space. The glow that radiates from you puts everyone at ease. Your laughter is extremely contagious! You always know exactly what to say and when to say it. Your words of wisdom and encouragement have guided me through many of life's challenges. I always leave your presence in a better state than when I arrived. I am so grateful to know you and to call you my friend!

Love Always,

Cheryl Bauman

I STILL REMEMBER the day I met Georgia. A fellow yogini, Laurel Anderson (RIP), who had heard that I was looking for more opportunities to teach chair yoga, invited me to contact Georgia as she had heard that she was looking to train and hire new teachers. I met her at a retirement home in South Ottawa and watched as she cheerfully and enthusiastically managed to combine a plethora of music with individual chair yoga movements. What I admired most about her was her energy, kindness and big smile, but I also loved her very eclectic and Bohemian style. Dressed in a purple shirt, long purple and green earrings, and lots of rings and bracelets, I thought to myself: "Wow, she's not only offering yoga, but also bringing sunshine with glitter and gloss to their day!" We had a two-hour break between this class and the next, so we headed off to do some shopping at her favourite second-hand store. From one lover of thrift stores to another, our friendship solidified as I loved that she was so down to earth, kind, and a bit flaky! Twenty years later, we are still friends and have shared lunch at each other's houses on many occasions. Scattered across my windowsills, are small rocks with the words "Acknowledge, Accept, Adjust" decorated by Georgia with hearts and friends holding hands.

Thanks for your gifts, Georgia
I love you to the moon and back.

Terri Morgan
Yoga Therapist and Instructor

It is not possible to put into words how much Georgia means to our family. Every interaction any of us has with her always leaves a lasting warmth. Her selfless love, joy, and genuine care never go unnoticed. The sun may rise and set from east to west, but Georgia's gift for making people smile never takes a rest.

The Wilsons

From Budapest to the Maple Tree

A Poem for Georgia and Alan Morissette

In Budapest, where the Danube flows,
Where whispers ride the winds that blow,
A girl named Georgia dreamed one day
To find a life far, far away.

With heart held high and spirit wide,
She left her home, her past, her pride
To chase the dawn on distant shores,
Through hopeful tears and untold doors.

To Canada she came alone,
Yet never once did she bemoan.
For in her chest a fire burned
A will to build, to grow, to learn.

And there she met, like fate's own thread,
A gentle man with eyes of stead
Alan, calm as forest air,
With hands that knew both work
and care.

Together they carved out a song,
A life where roots grew deep and strong.
Three children rose like morning light:
Alanis bold, with voice so bright;
Wade, the rock with quiet grin;
And Chad, the spark that lives within.
Years passed on like pages turned,
Each wrinkle earned, each lesson learned.
And now with wisdom in her eyes,
Georgia lifts her gaze to skies.

A memoir stirs within her soul,
A tale of loss, of love, of goal.
Of what it means to leave behind,
Yet carry all you are in mind.

A book to hold the fire and frost,
The things she gained, the things
she lost.
Of Hungary's hills, and Canada's snow,
Of how a girl found strength to grow.

So write, dear Georgia, write it true,
The world needs stories told by you.
And Alan, standing by your side,
Will watch your journey's truths abide.

Your children read the lines you weave,
Of where you came, of why you leave.
A legacy in ink and heart
A brave woman's immortal art.

Jackie Sabourin

I HAD JUST completed my Yoga Teacher training in 2012 and heard about chair yoga. We can all benefit from this practice, no matter what age or shape we are in. This really inspired me to find out more, so I reached out to a friend who gave me Georgia's name and contact information. I called her and we had a positive conversation, which led her to become my mentor. This was the beginning of our journey, which is still flourishing as I write this. We have a beautiful friendship and our life paths are similar in many ways. Georgia helped me bring out the best version of myself, the freedom to be me. She is the one who saw greatness even when I didn't see it in myself.

Namaste,

Barbara Fulford

GEORGIA'S INFECTIOUS POSITIVITY and love for encouraging others have truly inspired me to be more proactive about engaging in random acts of kindness. Whether she's lighting up a senior home with her joyful chair yoga, or brightening a stranger's day with a simple note, Georgia truly demonstrates how small gestures can make a big impact on those that she encounters. She's a beautiful example of someone who spreads light wherever she goes.

Mike McMain

OVER FIFTY YEARS have passed, and her lessons of kindness have never faded, for either of us. You see, it's not impossible for a student and his fifth-grade teacher to touch each other's souls. Mrs. Morissette was arguably the most instrumental teacher in my early development. We can only describe Mrs. Morissette as a fantastic, kind teacher with a lot of skill, who brought out the best in us. She was my teacher at St. Bernard's Catholic School, class of 1974–1975. I was an eleven-year-old boy with a lot of questions... and answers too, or so he thought. Mrs. Morissette created a class project to have us write a form-style letter and seek out companies that we wanted to learn more about. The class contacted many companies and a bunch of us even received replies. So cool! Then came a call for me down at the office. Me! Pure Spring Bottling Company was on the phone. They were impressed by our lesson plan. So impressed that a Pure Spring truck arrived a few days later with drinks for the whole school, and I got to keep the returns! That lesson has been incorporated into many of my business successes to this day.

Now I could end the story here, and just say she was a great teacher, which she was, but there's more. Mrs. Morissette came to class and mentioned she needed a babysitter for her new twins and eldest son. Without hesitation, I asked her for permission to go to the office to call my mom, and off I went. At the end of the day, my mom came to pick me up and told Mrs. Morissette she spoke to me and was here to help with the kids. Mom even offered Mrs. Morissette her car to get to school. For the next two years, Diane (my mom) and her family were part of the Morissette home. Great lessons in love, caring, and ginger ale! And kindness paid back to a great teacher. Indelible memories of a wonderful teacher and a great mom.

J. Frank Papineau

Heart of the House
by Alanis Morissette

An Unexpected Afterword

WE ALL KNOW that, over an entire lifespan, there will be times when we do not have control over what happens to us.

To conclude, I would like to share the health challenge life has recently thrown my way. My memoirs have described many recurring themes in my life, and one of those has always been to find the gift hidden or buried inside hardship and adversity.

In the summer of 2024, I was diagnosed with uterine cancer. After surgery, I was told that it was stage 1A. The surgery was a success. At first, it was a bit of a shock, but then we started looking for the silver lining, the positive, the gifts that could be drawn from such an ordeal. The belief that there is always hope came flashing into my mind and helped me face this trial. Fortunately, my emotional strength and my positive attitude prevented me from getting depressed or from going down any dark rabbit hole. The first gift was my husband's and my three children's support. The second, the love I received from the many friends I have who clearly demonstrated their care and attention. The third and final gift was the close and new friendships of the medical team that cared for me and supported a plan of treatment and recovery.

As of June 2025, I no longer had any signs of cancer cells spreading. I did my research. I listened to my body and reviewed the fact that it was a stage 1A cancer located deep inside the uterus wall. I heard my enemy was an aggressive cancer, but there were no lymph nodes near the mass. In the "war room" of my mind, I expanded my defence team of Canadian doctors, American doctors, as well as some individuals with no clinical accreditation. We went to war with the weapons of our choice, which included medications that were not approved in my home country, but which had shown great results around the world. I was determined to strengthen my artillery of positivity and patience and had faith that together we would win out.

After a successful hysterectomy, and together with my body's messages, wise advice from doctors, and support from family and friends, I was able to quickly get back into the flow of my regular productive life and routine.

I am now in remission and on a mission to stay cancer free.

So Alive
by Wade Morissette

Endorsement

Why Should People Read this Book

A Recommendation by Dr. Cheryl Bauman, Registered Life Coach and Published Author

HER STORY [IS] an inspiring narrative of a lifetime full of trials and triumphs. Georgia is a living, breathing, transformational masterpiece. She had made the choice to fully surrender to her purpose-filled life and calling of service through the promotion of well-being, despite the many obstacles, with which she had to contend. Georgia continues to accomplish her life-given assignments by allowing both the challenges and the victories to mould her into an extraordinary human being. This exceptional author has blessed countless people, including myself, through the wisdom and knowledge she has gained and readily shares. You too can be changed by the life-giving energy found in this book—it is contagious. I encourage you to accept Georgia's wise counsel, as you will always become a better person.

Duo

A New Imprint Dedicated to Literary Works and Ideas

Duo presents works of fiction and non-fiction, in French and in English, as well as in Indigenous languages, from established writers and emerging talents. It is one of the imprints of Les Presses de l'Université d'Ottawa / University of Ottawa Press (PUO-UOP).

Other Literary Titles Published by the University of Ottawa Press

Literary Works

Michel Bastarache, *Bien assis*, 2026.
Roseann O'Reilly Runte, *Renshi*, 2026.
Hélène Koscielniak, *Et si...*, 2026.
Denis Bachand, *L'énigme du carnet rouge*, 2026.
Marie-Claude Thifault (ed.), *La vie : c'est comme une bicyclette, il faut avancer pour ne pas perdre l'équilibre*, foreword by Florence Khoriaty, 2026.
Tareyn Johnson, *Dawaa: The Space in Between*, 2026.
Abla Farhoud, *Happiness Has a Slippery Tail*, translated from the French by Judith Weisz Woodsworth, 2025.
Jean-Louis Grosmaire, *Mouvance et espérance*, 2025.
Yolande Bastarache, *Détresse et nostalgie*, 2024.
Robert Major, *Éloge de la procrastination et autres facéties*, 2022.
Michel Picard, *Kilis*, 2021.
Jean-Louis Grosmaire, *Acadissima*, 2021. Prix France-Acadie.
Yolande Bastarache, *Mon village*, la côte, 2021.
Maurice Henrie, *Odette*, 2020.
Michel Picard, *Memoriam*, 2020.
Camilla Grudova, *L'alphabet des poupées*, translated from the English by Véronique Lessard and Marc Charron, 2020.
Maurice Henrie, *La maison aux lilas*, 2019.
Andrew F. Sullivan, *Tout vient à mourir*, translated from the English by Marc-André Clément, 2017.

Literary Non-fiction

Thomas Burelli, Alexandre Lillo, Lauren Touchant, Lynda Hubert Ta, and Elie Klee, *30 Climate COPs Later: Stories from Canadian Participants*, 2025.

Pierre Calvé, *Le français grandeur nature : portrait et défense d'une langue vivante*, 2025.

Nicole V. Champeau, *Pointe Maligne, retrouvée par les textes* : présence française dans le Haut Saint-Laurent (tome II), 2023.

Robert Major, *Identité, appartenances : un parcours franco-ontarien*, 2023.

Maurice Henrie, *La tête haute*, 2022. Prix du livre d'Ottawa.

Denis Bachand, *Voyages en nostalgie : parcours mémoriel à travers les arts et les médias*, 2021.

Robert Major, *Témiscamingue : châtiments, miracles, et autres propos du concierge de l'évêché*, 2021.

Robert Major, *Carnets du rang 5 : fragments d'un enracinement, fragments d'un parcours*, 2021.

Robert Major, *Mes conversations avec Claude*, 2019.

Biographies and Memoirs

Harvey Sawler, *Quest for Beauty: The Photographic Journey of Malak of Ottawa*, 2026.

Benjamin Maiangwa, *One Boy! A Boarding School Memoir*, 2026.

Paul-François Sylvestre, *Lys, trillium et arc-en-ciel : doublement minoritaire*, 2025.

John Symon and Stéphane Desjardins, Bob Silverman: *The Impossible Hero / Bob Silverman : vélorutionnaire*, 2025.

Monique Aubry-Frize, *Une femme en ingénierie : mémoires d'une pionnière*, translated from the English by Suzanne Aubry, 2024.

Roy MacGregor, *L'étoile du nord : le mystère éternel de Tom Thomson et de la femme qui l'aimait*, translated from the English by Benoit Léger, 2023.

Fred Langan, *Elle a osé réussir : biographie de l'honorable Marie-P. Charette-Poulin / She Dared to Succeed: A Biography of the Honourable Marie-P. Charette-Poulin*, 2023.

Michel Bastarache and Antoine Trépanier, *What I Wish I Had Told My Children*, translated from the French by Julie Da Silva, 2023.

Stéphane Desjardins, *La famille Fermanian : l'histoire du cinéma Pine de Sainte-Adèle*, 2022.

Michel Bastarache and Antoine Trépanier, *Michel Bastarache : ce que je voudrais dire à mes enfants*, 2019.

Discover Duo and all works of fiction and literary non-fiction here:
duoeditions.ca

For a complete list of titles published by the University of Ottawa Press, please visit:
www.Press.uOttawa.ca

www.ingramcontent.com/pod-product-compliance
Lightning Source LLC
LaVergne TN
LVHW050206130926
847810LV00035B/426